edexcel

CW01652966

Edexcel AS History U

Russia in Revolution 1881-1924: From Autocracy to Dictatorship

Derrick Murphy

Series editors: Derrick Murphy and Angela Leonard

STUDENT BOOK

A PEARSON COMPANY

Contents

Introduction

Welcome to History at AS level. History is a fascinating subject, concerned with the world as it was and how it became the world we know now. By studying history, you will encounter new people, new places, new societies and cultures – even though they are all in the past! If you have an enquiring mind and an interest in the world around you then History is the subject for you.

How to make the most of the course

- Practise your skills. History is not just about learning information or about telling the story of what happened in the past. You need to be able to understand and explain *why* things turned out the way they did and about how much they changed. The skills builder sections in this book will help you do this.
- Prepare for debate and discussion! Historians do not always agree about why events or developments in the past happened, or about their importance – so don't be afraid to debate with your teacher and other students. But remember that you must give evidence to support any point you make.
- Use the course book. This book has been designed to help you build up the skills, knowledge and understanding to help you do well in you exam – so use it! See the 'How this book will help you' section for details.
- Read around the subject. The more you learn about a period of history, the more interesting it becomes. Further reading on your chosen topics will broaden your understanding of the period, give you better insights into causation and change and make the course much more rewarding.

What you will learn

Unit 1 focuses on historical themes in breadth. This means that you need to be able to understand and explain why things changed over a fairly long period of time. In Option D3 you will learn about how and why Russia changed from being ruled by a monarch with absolute power and became the world's first communist state. You will examine how the Russian monarchy faced and dealt with threats to its position, about how weak rulers and war shook its foundations and how revolution brought about its demise. You will find out how the Russian Revolution came about, how the Communists took over, and how one man, Lenin, rose above other potential leaders to create the Union of Soviet Socialist Republics, or the USSR.

How you will be assessed

For Unit 1, you will take a written exam. You will write two essays, one on each topic you have studied (i.e. one on Russia in Revolution and one on your other chosen topic). For each topic you will have a choice of two questions. You will have one hour and 20 minutes in total, or 40 minutes for each essay.

How this book will help you

- Clearly written text gives you the historical information you need for this topic in the right amount of depth.
- 'Take note' boxes indicate when you should make notes of your own. These notes will help you with the activities and can also form the basis of your revision so it's worth keeping up to date with these as you go along.
- Activities help you understand the content and build up your historical skills.
- Skills builder sections help you develop the essential skills you need to do well in your exam.
- Examzone tells you what you need to know to prepare for the exam, including:
  - What to expect on the day
  - How to revise
  - What the assessment objectives mean and how you can meet them
  - What the different levels mean and how you can gain a high mark
  - Example essays with examiner commentaries to help you understand what the examiners are looking for and how to use your information.

Chapter 1 Russia before 1881

Key questions

- What was Russia like in 1881?
- How had Alexander II (1855–1881) brought change to Russia?
- What factors brought change in Russia in the period 1881–1924?

In 1881 Russia was one of Europe's five Great Powers, along with Britain, France, Germany and Austria–Hungary. It dominated eastern Europe and was a major force in European international relations. However, Russia was more than just a European state – it was vast, covering large areas of Asia as well as Europe. Russia was also Europe's most conservative state – the centre of anti-revolutionary and anti-liberal ideas. But by 1924 Russia was transformed. It had become the world's most radical state, its first communist society, with a mission for world revolution. The process by which Russia changed from a conservative autocracy to a communist dictatorship is the main theme of this book.

Rulers of Russia

1801–1825	Tsar Alexander I	Absolute Monarchy
1825–1855	Tsar Nicholas I	Absolute Monarchy
1855–1881	Tsar Alexander II	Absolute Monarchy
1881–1894	Tsar Alexander III	Absolute Monarchy
1894–1917	Tsar Nicholas II	Absolute Monarchy
1917 February to July	Prince Lvov	Provisional Government
July to October	Alexander Kerensky	Provisional Government
1917–1924	Lenin	Communist Government

The rulers of Russia before 1855 were regarded as reactionary autocrats, unwilling to consider any political or social change. Then Alexander II received the title of 'Tsar Liberator' because he instituted important political and social reforms. Alexander III, however, reverted to the pre-1855 type of reactionary autocrat. Nicholas II was then forced to make political changes because of the 1905 Revolution. But the only period of democratic-style rule was under the Provisional Government, for when Lenin assumed power he reintroduced a dictatorial style of government.

Autocracy

Autocracy was the system of government in Russia, under the Tsars. The Tsar had no limits on his power and was accountable to no one but God. It was believed that he was divinely appointed and that God supported his actions. One of the Tsar's strongest supporters was the official State Church, the Russian Orthodox Church. The Tsar had advisers, but he was not bound to listen to their advice, and laws were made by 'ukase' (imperial decree).
This total power made the Romanov dynasty, which ruled Russia from 1613 to 1917, the most powerful in Europe.

The world's largest state

Tsarist Russia was the largest continuous land empire in modern history, covering one sixth of the world's surface. Russia stretched from Poland and the Baltic Sea in the west to the Pacific Ocean in the east. From 1789 it even included Alaska in North America, until 1867, when it was sold to the USA. It was over 5000 miles from the capital, St Petersburg, to Vladivostok in the far east. Before the 1890s and the extension of the railway system east

Timeline

1855	Alexander II becomes Tsar	
1861	Emancipation of the serfs	
1881	Alexander II assassinated. His successor, Alexander III, begins a period of repression	
1892	Witte becomes Finance Minister. The 'Great Spurt' of industrial growth begins	
1894	Nicholas II becomes Tsar	
1898	Social Democrat Party founded	
1901	Social Revolutionary Party founded	
1904	Outbreak of Russo-Japanese War	
1905	Year of Revolution	
1906	Stolypin becomes Prime Minister	
1911	Stolypin assassinated	
1914	Outbreak of the First World War	
1917	February:	Revolution – the Tsar abdicates, and the Provisional Government is established
	April:	Lenin returns to Russia; April Theses
	July:	July Days
	August:	Kornilov Affair
	October:	Bolshevik seizure of power; Lenin establishes new government
1918	Outbreak of the Civil War. 'War Communism' introduced	
1921	Civil War ends Kronstadt Mutiny 'New Economic Policy' replaces War Communism	
1922	Creation of the USSR. Lenin becomes seriously ill	
1924	Lenin dies	

of Moscow, it could take months to travel from St Petersburg to Vladivostok. Although vast in extent, much of the Empire was of limited productive use because of its geography and climate.

Geography

The Russian Empire could be divided, from north to south, into zones of vegetation, as shown on the map. In the far north was the tundra, an area of grassland which was permanently frozen. It was inhabited by tribes who were related to the Inuit. South of the tundra was the taiga, a vast belt of coniferous forest. Next came a belt of deciduous forest, and in the southern part of the Empire was a vast plain, the steppe, in the west. This was the main crop-growing area. In the Asian part of the Empire, however, the most southern belt was desert and semi-desert which spread as far as the Himalayas.

In addition, the Empire possessed several mountain ranges. The Urals divided European from Asiatic Russia. On the borders of Turkey, between the Black and Caspian Seas, were the Caucasus mountains. The tundra, desert and mountainous regions could sustain little human activity. However, the taiga offered the potential for hunting and timber, while the broad grasslands of the steppe were 'the breadbasket of the Empire'.

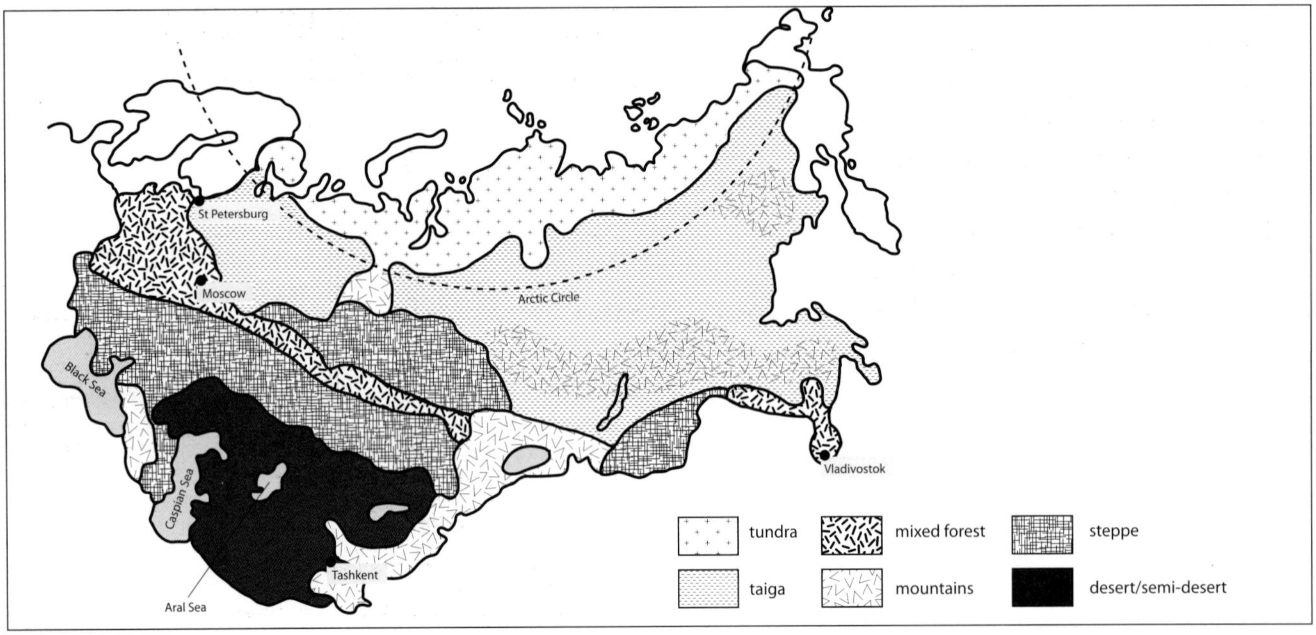

Physical map of Russia showing different belts of vegetation.

The economy

Russia was an overwhelmingly rural country, with agriculture as the mainstay of the economy. Agriculture had to feed Russia's large and growing population – it grew from 56 million in 1831 to 98 million in 1881. Grain was also Russia's most valuable export, much of it being shipped from the Black Sea port of Odessa. Although Russia had immense natural resources, such as iron ore and coal, the country's industrial development was modest, and limited to towns such as St Petersburg, Moscow and parts of the Ukraine.

Take note

1. Using the information in this section, provide reasons for why Russia was regarded as a 'backward' state in the nineteenth century.
2. Find reasons why you think the Russian Empire was a difficult country to govern in the nineteenth century.

Society

Russian society in the nineteenth century had changed little over the previous hundred years. At the top of society was the Tsar, who had absolute political power and owned vast estates across Russia. Beneath the Tsar was the Court, containing leading landowners and members of the government. This privileged group, which was supported by the leading members of the Russian Orthodox Church, comprised the ruling elite and possessed considerable social and political power. Below the Court was a small group of businessmen and traders, who were supported by a small class of industrial workers.

The vast majority of the Russian population, before 1861, consisted of state peasants and serfs. Serfdom had developed in Russia in the fifteenth century, as an essential part of what was regarded as the 'service state'. Nobles owed allegiance to the Tsar and, in return for their support, the serfs were tied to the land owned by the nobles. Serfs owed a variety of obligations to their owners. Some (barschina serfs) worked a number of days a week for their master, while others (obrok serfs) paid rent.

Landowners had considerable power over serfs, including the power to administer justice, with only capital punishment being forbidden. Serfs could not leave the land without permission from the landowners. Although they controlled serfs' lives, the landowners did not technically own them.

Serfs were legally tied to the land and the landowners owned the land. It's important to understand this connection, as it is the reason that freed serfs were required to pay redemption payments for the land after emancipation. This was a source of deep resentment for the serfs. Although nobles were freed from state service in 1762, it took until 1861 for the serfs to be freed from service.

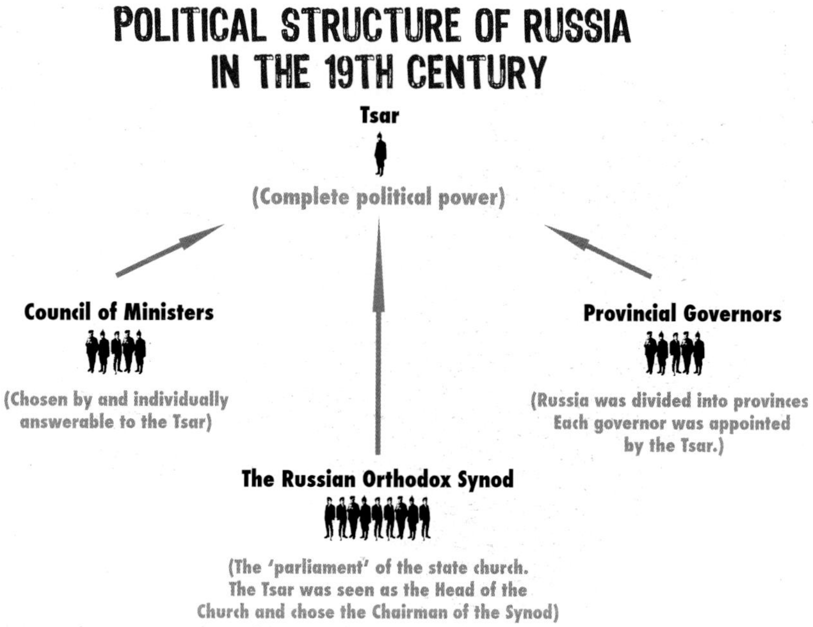

A multiracial Empire

Although known as the 'Russian' Empire, the state was made up of a wide variety of ethnic groups. The largest and most powerful were the Russians, centred on the area between St Petersburg and Moscow. In European Russia there were also Finns, Estonians, Latvians, Lithuanians, Poles, Ukrainians and Belorussians. In the Caucasus area were Georgians, Armenians and Azeris. And in Asiatic Russia were Turkmens, Uzbeks, Kazakhs, Tajiks and Tartars.

The Empire also had a variety of religions. The most powerful was the Russian Orthodox Church, which was the official religion. But in the west there were Catholics, in Asia a significant number of Muslims, and in northern Russia there were Animists.

The legacy of the 'Tsar Liberator', Alexander II, 1855–1881

The emancipation of the serfs, 1861

The biggest social problem facing Russia in the mid-nineteenth century was serfdom. Approximately eighty per cent (25 million) of the Russian population were serfs or state peasants. The vast majority of serfs were landless peasants. For generations before the reign of Alexander II, the existence of serfdom was recognised as the major obstacle to the modernisation of Russian society. It led to subsistence agriculture – which meant that serfs produced only enough food to feed themselves. Very little produce was available for export, and in times of poor harvest there was widespread famine.Serfdom had existed elsewhere in Europe at the beginning of the nineteenth century, but by 1855 Russia was the only major power which still kept serfdom. Eventually, in 1861, Alexander II issued a ukase (imperial decree) which abolished serfdom.

This did not mean, however, that the former serfs were completely free. They had been tied to the land – and the owners of that land now had to be compensated by the State. As a result, the former serfs had to pay 'redemption payments' (taxes) to the Russian government – for forty-nine years. In addition, serfs were forced to live in 'mirs' (communes) where land was held collectively. The mirs were administered by elders of the community. Periodically, the elders would redistribute land within the mir, according to need, a policy that acted as a major obstacle to agricultural improvement. Also, if a peasant wanted to leave the mir, he or she would have to get the elders' permission. These developments greatly impeded the modernisation of Russian agriculture. The system also obstructed the movement of people into towns, impeding the development of industry. In the second half of the nineteenth century, matters were made worse by the rapid rise in population in European Russia. The combined effect of all these changes was to create periodic shortages of food, which occasionally became full-scale famines

Political and judicial reform

In 1864 the Tsar Liberator, Alexander II, introduced the first form of elective government in Russian history, although the electorate was limited to the educated and the wealthy. These local government units in rural areas were known as zemstva (singular: zemstvo). Their powers were limited to functions such as elementary education and road building. In 1870 elective local government was extended to towns and cities.

In 1870 the Tsar's government modernised the Russian judicial system and introduced trial by jury This meant that ordinary Russians participated in the dispensation of justice, whereas before 1870 justice had been the preserve of the Tsar's officials.

> **Take note**
>
> Write down a list of reforms passed during the reign of Alexander II.

The main themes in Russian history

Change from above

Russia had a strong tradition of political, social and economic change from above, meaning change brought about by rulers or the government. In the early eighteenth century a major period of change was brought about by Tsar Peter the Great. In 1855 to 1881 Alexander II also launched another period of change. From 1917 to 1924, Lenin also forced through reform from above. This was due in the main to the fact that Russian politics was not democratic for most of its existence. It was ruled either by Tsarist autocrats or Communist dictators. Under both systems political power was firmly in the hands of the rulers.

> **Take note**
>
> Study the timeline on page 6 and this information on the main themes in Russian history. Link events within the timeline to the themes.

War

Change was also brought about as a result of war. From 1854 to 1856, Russia fought Britain, France and Turkey in the Crimean War, much of the fighting taking place on Russian soil. Russia's defeat was the major reason for Alexander II's reforms in the 1860s. From 1904 to 1905, Russia fought Japan in a war over territory in the Far East. Russian defeat in this war helped fuel revolution at home during 1905. Finally, Russian involvement in the First World War placed huge social and economic strains on the Empire as it struggled to fight a European War against Germany, Austria–Hungary and Turkey. Russian defeats undermined the authority of the Tsar and, combined with the economic crisis, helped to bring him down in the February Revolution of 1917.

The decision of the Provisional Government (February–October 1917) to continue fighting in the war, in turn, undermined its authority and assisted the Bolshevik seizure of power. Finally, the Civil War of 1918 to 1921 resulted in major political and economic change under the Bolsheviks. War Communism was introduced and 'political terror' became part of the way that the Bolsheviks maintained their power.

Revolution

Another key feature of Russian history was political change through revolution. In 1905 the Revolution resulted in the October Manifesto which allowed the creation of Russia's first elected national parliament, the Duma.

In February 1917 the Revolution resulted in the abdication of the Tsar and the end of the 300 years of rule by the Romanov family. It also led to a brief period of liberal, democratic government under the Provisional Government. The October Revolution of 1917 brought about the creation of the world's first communist state and led to a transformation in the social, economic and political structure of Russia.

Activity: Alexander II's reforms

Study the reforms passed by Alexander II and place them in order of importance, giving reasons for your choice.

Activity: Life in Russia

You are a visitor to Russia from western Europe in 1881.You have to write a short article for a British newspaper on life in Russia in 1881. Remember to give your article a headline, and mention each of the important points in a separate paragraph.

A Russian village in the late 19th century

Chapter 2 The triumph of reaction – the reign of Alexander III, 1881–1894

Key questions

- What problems did Alexander III face when he became Tsar?
- How did Alexander III deal with threats to Russian autocracy?
- How far did Alexander III bring political and social change to Russia?

On 13 March 1881, Tsar Alexander II, while travelling through St Petersburg, was assassinated by a terrorist group called the 'People's Will', a radical group opposed to the autocratic rule of the Tsars. What is perhaps surprising was the fact that the Tsar was on his way to sign a law which would have given Russia its first national assembly. Tsar Alexander II had been given the title 'Tsar Liberator' for his radical reform during his reign from 1855 to 1881. His most important reform was the emancipation of the serfs, in 1861.

His son, Alexander III, therefore became Tsar, in the most tragic and untimely of circumstances. The immediate impact of Alexander III's rise to power was the end of any further political reform. Instead, his reign is noted for being one of political repression. Unfortunately, through their assassination of the reformist Alexander II, the People's Will had created their worst nightmare – a truly repressive Tsar.

Rulers of Russia

Alexander II	1855–1881
Alexander III	1881–1894
Nicholas II	1894–1917

The problems facing Alexander III in 1881

When Alexander III became Tsar, Russia was in crisis following the assassination of Alexander II. Supreme political authority was still in the hands of the Tsar, but there were immense challenges facing Alexander III as he suddenly became Tsar of the world's largest country, covering a quarter of the world's land surface. Although known as the 'Russian' Empire, it comprised a large number of ethnic groups, with the Russians making up only half the population. It was the Russians, however, who completely dominated the political and economic system.

Alexander III faced the problem of keeping this large multi-ethnic empire together. At the same time, he needed to maintain his own supreme political power – which was difficult, because his father, Alexander II, had begun reforms which raised expectations of major change within Russia.

Russia was also one of Europe's Great Powers, and Alexander III faced pressures from some of his advisers to reform his empire to make it more

Take note

As you read through the following sections on 'The problems facing Alexander III' and 'Repression and reaction' make yourself two sets of cards, one for each section. On each of your 'problem cards' should be a problem facing Alexander III in 1881, with a brief description. On each of your 'policy cards' write a policy introduced by Alexander III to deal with the problems he faced.

Timeline

1881	Alexander II assassinated by the People's Will Alexander III becomes Tsar Repression of radical political groups Russification becomes major government policy
1884	Peasant Land Bank created Primary schools placed under Church control
1887	Assassination attempt on Alexander III by the People's Will
1889	Creation of Land Captains
1891	Famine in European Russia
1894	Alexander III dies, aged 49

like western and central Europe. This would involve reforming the autocracy, allowing an elective parliament to share political power with the Tsar. People who held these views were known as 'Westerners'. Other advisers – known as Slavophiles – suggested that Russia develop along its own unique lines. They wanted the Empire to be autocratic and dominated by the Russians because, they believed, it was the authority of the Tsar that held this large and diverse Empire together.

How could Alexander III restore order, and set Russia on a course of political, social and economic stability?

Part of Alexander III's problem was the legacy left by his father. The assassination of the father horrified Russian society – and appalled his son. Throughout most of his adult life the future Alexander III had not been involved in politics. However, he had made it known that he did not approve of his father's modernising policies, and in 1881, when he became Tsar, he launched Russia on a return to conservatism and so brought an end to further political reform.

By the 1870s it seemed that Russia was on the road to becoming a modern European state similar to the other Great Powers such as Germany and Austria–Hungary. Amongst the educated classes it was felt that the emancipation of the serfs and political and judicial reform would be the beginning of major political change, which would end the Tsarist autocracy in national government. The reforms already included the creation of elective local government, the zemstva, in 1864, and trial by jury in 1870.

But the rise in expectation was dashed by the restrictions placed on the freed serfs and the modest nature of political reform. As a result, disillusioned radicals amongst the educated classes began to believe that the only way to truly modernise Russia would be the eradication of Tsarism itself. The organisation 'People's Will' was formed, in 1879, for this purpose. Throughout the late 1870s senior Tsarist officials were murdered. The ultimate act against the Tsarist system was to assassinate the Tsar himself. Between 1879 and 1880 four unsuccessful attempts were made on the Tsar's life. Ironically, in 1881 when Alexander II was assassinated he was on his way to sign a decree to allow a form of elective national government.

Glossary: Great Power

A Great Power was defined by its military power. As armed forces became large and more expensive to maintain, by the late nineteenth century military power was becoming increasingly linked to economic power.

Alexander II's key reforms

The zemstva reform, 1864: For the first time in Russian history, an elective form of government was created. Zemstva were limited to rural areas. They had responsibility for elementary education and road building. They were elected by the educated and wealthy. In 1870 elective local government was extended to towns and cities.

Trial by jury, 1870: Before 1870 trials were decided by a judge appointed by a Provincial Governor. From 1870 trials were decided by juries made up of ordinary Russians.

Repression and reaction

The assassination of the Tsar threatened the entire social and political system of the Russian Empire. At the top were members of the landed aristocracy and senior members of the Russian Orthodox Church. The aristocracy did not have popular support from the Russian people and the senior members of the Russian Orthodox Church derived much of their power from the Tsar, so a threat to the Tsar meant a threat to their position as well. So when Alexander III launched a campaign of repression it had widespread support from the upper levels of Russian society and from Slavophiles.

A cartoon published by Russian socialists in 1900 showing their interpretation of Russian society under the tsars. From the bottom, the poster shows the workers, saying 'We work for nothing and...', the army 'they shoot at us', the capitalists 'they dine out on our behalf', and the clergy 'they pray on our behalf', the tsar and his court 'they spend our money'.

How does this representation help us understand the social structure of Russia in the late 19th and early 20th century? What message is the cartoon trying to send out?

Take note

What actions did Alexander III's government take to deal with political unrest?

Political repression

In Russia, those who wanted reform ranged from moderates to extremists. Moderates included liberals who supported peaceful political change. Liberals wanted to allow freedom of the press and a national parliament elected by the educated and wealthy.

Extremism took many forms. Some, like People's Will, were nihilists – they just wanted to destroy the Tsar's rule and give power to the people without any clear plan as to how this might work in practice. Others wanted political and economic power handed to the peasants. In areas like Poland, nationalists wanted to create their own national state, outside the Russian Empire. The one thing they all had in common was the desire to change the political system. And to Alexander III, it was clear that all those who supported political reform should be repressed.

Tsarist Russia, as shown by the 1897 Census (%)

Ruling class (Tsar and government)	0.5
Upper class (Landed classes, higher clergy)	12.0
Middle class (merchants, factory owners, etc.)	1.5
Industrial working class	4.0
Peasants	82.0

Konstantin Pobedonostsev

(1827–1907)

Leading thinker of Russian conservatism and an ardent defender of the Tsarist autocracy. Professor of Civil Law at the University of Moscow in 1858. From 1880 he became Procurator of the Holy Synod of the Russian Orthodox Church. As such, he was the government's leading official on religious policy. He was tutor to both Alexander III and Nicholas II when they were children.

The first casualties in the campaign of repression were Alexander II's liberal ministers, M.T. Loris-Melikov and N.P. Ignatiev, who left office. In their place came Konstantin Pobedonostsev, Chief Procurator of the Holy Synod of the Russian Orthodox Church. As the Tsar's chief minister and leading official of the State Church, Pobedonostsev wielded immense power and influence. He was the person who masterminded Alexander III's Manifesto, which was issued at the end of April 1881 – just five weeks after the Tsar Liberator's assassination.

The Manifesto declared that absolute political power resided in the Tsar. An unbending conservative, Pobedonostsev believed the basis of political and social stability lay in support for autocracy, the Russian Orthodox Church and Russian nationalism.

However, the immediate task of Alexander III's new government was to destroy the terror organisation, the People's Will. In the wake of the assassination, the government introduced the Statute of State Security, which set up government-controlled courts to try government opponents. The government could now arrest and put on trial political opponents, without the need for a jury. Those convicted faced possible execution, and thousands were exiled to Siberia. Although these courts, which helped maintain political stability, were only meant as a temporary measure, they stayed in existence until the end of the Tsarist autocracy in 1917.

The government also took action to prevent the spread of radical – and even liberal – ideas. Press freedom was severely restricted, with fourteen major newspapers being banned between 1882 and 1889 for displaying 'liberal' tendencies. Foreign books and newspapers were also rigorously censored by the Okhrana (the secret police) in order to prevent dangerous foreign ideas – such as democracy and parliamentary government – reaching the Russian people.

The universities were a particular area singled out for strict government supervision. University fees were increased to exclude all but the very wealthy, and in 1884 the universities lost their self-government and came under government control. Universities across Russia were temporarily closed in 1889 because of student demonstrations against government control.

However, these repressive policies did not destroy the People's Will and other extremist groups. They continued to operate underground, and in 1887 they even made an attempt to assassinate Alexander III. In the crackdown that followed, the Okhrana arrested, and subsequently executed, a university student called Alexander Ulyanov – the elder brother of the future Bolshevik leader, Vladimir Ulyanov, better known as Lenin. In April 1917 Lenin wrote an eight-line autobiography which stated:

Increased central control

No aspect of Russian society seemed untouched by central government control. Pobedonostsev began to undo many of the reforms introduced by Alexander II. In 1889 the government created the post of 'Land Captain' to enforce local laws, replacing the locally elected justices of peace. Land Captains were members of the landed classes and were directly appointed by the Minister of the Interior.

In the following year, 1890, Land Captains were made members of the local government bodies – the zemstva. In addition, the franchise to the zemstva was restricted, to ensure that the landed classes had the most political power. Doctors and schoolteachers, for instance, were no longer allowed to seek election. In 1892 these restrictions were extended to towns and cities.

All these changes reversed many of Alexander II's reforms of 1855–1881. Russia was now the most repressive state in all Europe – with strict press censorship, virtually no legal political activity and wide-ranging police powers to deal with all those who criticised the Tsarist autocracy.

One area of particular interest to Pobedonostsev was religious control over education. He put all zemstva primary schools under Church control, and introduced restrictions to ensure that the sons of peasants and workers did not have the opportunity to enter secondary school.

The government also interfered with the trial by jury system, after a radical extremist, Vera Zasulich, was acquitted in a jury trial in 1878. She had shot dead the hated police chief of St Petersburg in broad daylight, but the jury's verdict reflected widespread public dislike of the repressive policies introduced under Alexander III. To prevent any further 'wrong' verdicts, from 1890 the government exercised the right to choose juries.

By the time of Alexander III's death, in 1894, Pobedonostsev had turned the clock back in terms of social and political reform. Much of the work of the Tsar Liberator had been undone. Russia was firmly back under the control of the Tsar, the landed classes and the Russian Orthodox Church.

The policy of Russification

Alexander III ruled over a multi-racial empire, and one way for him to bring unity and cohesion to even its far-flung corners was to adopt a policy of 'Russification' – insisting on the use of the Russian language. This policy had already been introduced late in the reign of the Tsar Liberator, but it reached new heights of implementation under Alexander III.

1. What problems did the Empire's multi-ethnic make-up create for the Tsar?

In 1885 Russian was made the official language for the whole Russian Empire. All official documents had to be in Russian, and all other languages were forbidden in schools – even where other races were in the majority. Areas which were badly affected by these developments were Poland and the Baltic lands of Estonia, Latvia and Lithuania. But the area

Nationalities in the Russian Empire, as shown by the 1897 Census (millions)

Russians	55.6
Ukrainians	22.4
Poles	7.9
Belarussians	5.8
Jews	5.2
Tartars	3.4
Germans	1.8
Armenians	1.2
Georgians	0.8

where this policy caused most resentment was Central Asia, where many people were not only non-Russian but also Muslim in religion.

It was the Jews, however, who suffered most under Alexander III. The majority of Russia's Jews lived in the 'Jewish Pale', which is now Belarus. Organised attacks on Jews greatly increased during the reign of Alexander III. These attacks – known as pogroms – would involve a mob going into Jewish parts of town to beat, rob, rape and even kill Jews. Under Alexander III, many of these attacks were organised or approved by the government. Such was the intensity of persecution in the early 1890s that thousands of Jews fled Russia for new lives in North America and western Europe.

Ivan Vyshnegradsky

(1831–1895)

Finance minister from 1887 to 1892. Previously known as a prominent scientist in the sphere of mechanical engineering and also as the author of several fundamental works and manuals. By the time he was appointed a government minister, his fortune amounted to nearly a million roubles. As finance minister, like his predecessor Nikolai Bunge, he pursued a policy aimed at settlement of the budget deficit, stronger government interference in the private railways, and monetary reform. In 1892 he was discharged from office for health reasons.

Financial reform

In 1881 Russia was one of the Great Powers of Europe. The others were Britain, France, Germany and Austria–Hungary. Although Russia was the largest, in terms of physical size and population, it was almost the most economically underdeveloped. Russia's economy was mainly based on agriculture, which was still quite backward and underproductive, making it difficult to sell enough grain at export to raise money for large-scale industrial development. If Russia wanted to maintain its position as a Great Power it would have to modernise its economy and increase its economic wealth in order to maintain its armed forces. Therefore, during Alexander III's reign, Russia embarked on important economic and financial reforms. Alexander III's first finance minister was Nikolai Bunge. In 1882 he introduced laws which reduced the tax burden on peasants. In the same year he established a Peasant Land Bank, which offered loan facilities to peasants to help them increase the size of their landholdings and make them more productive.

In 1887 Bunge resigned, to be replaced by Ivan Vyshnegradsky.

As peasants still farmed small strips of land, rather than large-scale farms, there was a high demand for land in European Russia. In 1889 Vyshnegradsky offered financial incentives for peasants to migrate to the eastern lands of Siberia. This took some pressure off the demand for land, but it couldn't prevent the catastrophic famine of 1891.

Of greater significance to the long-term economic development of Russia, Vyshnegradsky began to finance Russian economic development from foreign loans. By the late 1890s, most inward foreign investment in Russia came from France and Britain. It was during Vyshnegradsky's tenure of office that the foundations were laid for the rapid economic development of Russia which began in the 1890s under his successor as finance minister, Sergei Witte.

A truly repressive, autocratic state?

In October 1894, Alexander III died at the relatively young age of 49, of kidney disease, to be succeeded by his son, Nicholas II. During his reign, Alexander III had clearly re-established the autocratic power of the Tsar. This was based on the firm foundations of support from the landed classes and the Russian Orthodox Church. The whole social and political system was underpinned by the power of the Okhrana, backed by the might of the vast

Russian army. The Okhrana infiltrated extremist groups, arrested suspects, ran its own prisons and operated agents in foreign countries to spy on the activities of Russian political exiles. In many ways it was the forerunner of the Soviet secret police.

However, re-establishing the Tsar's authority had come at a cost. Political freedom was brutally suppressed, and the rights of ethnic and religious minorities were undermined in an empire dominated more and more by the Russian majority.

Many of the opponents of the Tsar had been arrested and exiled to Siberia. In 1895, a year after Alexander III's death, the future Bolshevik leader, Lenin, was arrested under emergency legislation and sent to Siberia for fourteen months imprisonment. Others had fled Russia to find refuge in western Europe. From there they continued to plot the downfall of the Tsarist regime.

The persecution of Jews forced many to join radical organisations, and in 1895 Jewish radicals formed their own left-wing organisation, the Bund, which later joined forces with Lenin's Bolsheviks.

The peasant population continued to grow, and their problems seemed to be worse than ever. Pressure on land use meant that the ever-increasing peasant population had less land per family to feed themselves. The famine of 1891 was followed by other famines in 1892 and 1893. The land issue in Russia seemed to be a time bomb, just waiting to explode into violent unrest in the early years of the twentieth century.

Activity: 'Continuity and change'

Identify the similarities and differences in Russia between the beginning and end of Alexander III's reign.

What do you regard as the most important difference?

The new Tsar: Nicholas II, 1894–1917

For an autocratic state to function effectively it requires clear direction from above. Alexander III had both vision and direction but, unfortunately, he was succeeded by a son who, at the age of 29, was noted for his indecision and his weakness. Nicholas was always regarded as 'soft' by his father. He had been given training in government affairs, but he showed very little interest. He had been advised by Pobedonostsev, who had given him a very narrow and conservative view of the vast empire that he inherited on his father's death.

Changes in Russia between 1881 and 1894

1881: On the eve of Alexander III's rule	1894: On Alexander III's death
Autocratic rule by the Tsar	Autocratic rule by the Tsar
Moderate political reform	Repression of political opponents
Backward economy	Financial and economic reform but economy still far behind other Great Powers
Violence by extremist groups	Political repression and secret police tackle extremist groups, but attacks still occur
Linguistic diversity across Empire	Policy of Russification – minorities suppressed

Nicholas II

(1868–1918)

Tsar from 1894 to 1917. He was a shy, quiet person who was eventually dominated by his wife, the Tsarina Alexandra. He was educated by tutors, the most important of whom was Konstantin Pobedonostsev, a brilliant philosopher, an arch-conservative and an opponent of political change. In many respects, the education of Nicholas was excellent. He had an unusual memory and had done well in history. He spoke French and German, and his English was good. Most of the time, as tsarevich (heir to the throne) Nicholas was required to do absolutely nothing – just wait until it was his turn to be tsar. And Alexander III, expecting that he would continue to occupy the throne for another twenty or thirty years, unfortunately put off giving his son the experience he would need to succeed him.

The historian Hans Rogger assessed the issue in 1983, when he wrote:

Tsar Nicholas II of Russia

Nicholas had no knowledge of the world or of men, of politics or government to help him make the difficult and weighty decisions that the Tsar alone must make.

The only guiding stars that he recognised were the inherited belief in the moral rightness of autocracy, and a religious faith that he was in God's hands, and his actions were divinely inspired.

(Hans Rogger, Russia in the Age of Modernisation and Revolution, 1983)

Nicholas II's accession to the throne had raised expectations that the oppression of Alexander III's reign might be relaxed. In January 1895 Nicholas II was visited by a delegation of zemstva who hoped for a more positive response to their plea for greater political responsibility. In his reply, Nicholas referred to their request as 'senseless dreams'. The new Tsar would face problems vastly greater than those faced by his father. Unfortunately, Nicholas II was not up to the task – and he would be the last Tsar of Russia.

Activity: Problems and policies

1. Using the cards you made for the 'Take note' on page 11 earlier, make links between the cards containing the problems Alexander III faced in 1881 and the cards with the policies he introduced. Try to match the 'problem cards' with the 'policy cards'.
2. Are there any policy cards without a match? If so, give a reason to support your view.
3. Arrange your policy cards in chronological order. Are there any policies which were more important at a particular time than others? Explain your answer.
4. Can you place the policies introduced under Alexander III in order of importance? Give reasons for your choices.

Chapter 3 Economic and social change – the age of Witte

Key questions

- Why was Russia economically and socially backward in the nineteenth century?
- Why did the Russian government embark on a programme of industrialisation in the 1890s?
- What impact did Witte's policies have on Russia?

In the late nineteenth century, Russia was one of Europe's Great Powers. This status had depended on military power but by the 1890s military power was becoming increasingly linked to economic power. Armies were vastly expensive – they were made up of millions of men, who were transported to war by railways and used advanced weaponry, such as machine guns. Of all the Great Powers, Russia was the most economically backward, with its wealth being based primarily on agriculture. However, the Russian Empire contained vast reserves of coal, oil and metals, and if it was to retain its position as a Great Power it had to exploit this enormous economic potential. In the 1890s, therefore, the Russian government embarked on an ambitious programme of economic modernisation. Under its Finance Minister, Sergei Witte, it planned to become one of the world's major economic powers.

The impact of emancipation

A major social and economic problem facing Russia before 1861 was serfdom. Approximately 80 per cent of the population were peasants and over half of these were serfs. Serfs were usually agricultural labourers who were tied to the land and were subject to extensive control by those who owned the land. During the early nineteenth century, Russia was plagued by unrest amongst the serf population. In addition, the system was seen as a major obstacle to economic development, because it encouraged subsistence agriculture which failed to produce the grain surpluses needed to create enough economic wealth for industrialisation. The 1861 ukase (imperial decree) ended the system by granting personal freedom to the serfs, along with ownership of their houses on their small plots. However, emancipation did not bring complete freedom. Former serfs had to pay redemption payments to the government over a period of 49 years. Also, former serfs were subject to control by their village communes, with village elders being able redistribute land between them, dependent on family size. And if a former serf wanted to leave a village he or she had to acquire permission from the village elders.

> **Take note**
>
> List the successes and problems arising from the emancipation of the serfs.

What made the problem worse was the rapid rise in growth of the Russian population, which doubled between 1861 and 1914 – to 130 million. As a result, much of the agricultural land in Russia was still engaged in subsistence agriculture. As late as 1880, only half of agricultural land was producing surpluses which could be sold. Although Russia was a vast

Take note

What were the main features of Witte's economic policy?

country, it had only a limited amount of productive agricultural land. Very few landowners could afford to become involved in agricultural improvement. Many of them had been in debt – in 1871 almost half the money given by the government to free the serfs was used by the landowners to pay off their mortgages and debts.

Glossary:

Tariffs

The taxes placed on imported goods to make them more expensive compared with home-produced goods. The policy of placing tariffs on imported goods is called protectionism.

Capital goods

Goods which are used to make consumer goods. Capital goods are regarded as vital if a country is to industrialise.

The 'Great Spurt' under Witte, 1892–1903

The person most associated with the rapid industrialisation of Russia in the 1890s was the Finance Minister, Sergei Witte. However, the foundations for growth were laid by his predecessors, Bunge and Vyshnegradsky. An important development was the introduction of high tariffs to protect the Russian economy in 1891.

Witte's aim was to make the Russian economy strong enough to maintain Russia's position as a Great Power. But Russia did not possess several of the factors required for the kind of rapid industrialisation taking place in Britain and Germany:

- Russia had a very small business class – the class that was central to the development of the British and other European economies in the nineteenth century.
- The majority of Russian peasants did not have complete freedom of movement, which limited the migration of workers to towns and cities to swell the workforce needed for new manufacturing industries.
- The Russian economy did not have sufficient funds to invest in industrial development. It couldn't produce enough surplus grain to raise the money necessary for industrialisation.

Count Sergei Witte

(1849–1915)

Witte was a Russian statesman, born in Georgia. He rose to high office through a rather unusual route – railway administration. He was Director of Railway Affairs within the Finance Ministry from 1889 to 1891, where he oversaw the building of the Trans-Siberian Railway. He was also unusual among senior government officials because he was sympathetic to the needs and aims of the business class. He was appointed Russian Finance Minister in 1892, and during his period in office the nation saw unprecedented economic growth. In 1903, he was transferred from the Finance Ministry to a lesser post.

As a result, Witte developed a plan for economic growth which differed from the rest of Europe. First, under the 'Witte system', economic development was sponsored and directed by the government. The government placed emphasis on the production of capital goods such as iron and steel, coal and machinery. Secondly, much of the economic development was financed from abroad, using massive inward investment from countries such as Belgium, France and Britain. And within Russia extra taxes were levied on the already over-taxed peasantry.

The centrepiece of the Witte system was a vast construction enterprise – the Trans-Siberian railway. The railway was to run 7000 km across the Empire, from the capital St Petersburg on the Baltic Sea to Vladivostock on the Pacific Ocean in the Far East. It would provide the communication system essential to exploit the economic potential of Siberia. In many ways it resembled the opening up of the West in the USA through the construction of the transcontinental railroad in the 1860s and 1870s.

The impact of the Witte system

The impact of Witte's policies were dramatic. Coal, iron and oil production all rose, and by 1903 much of the Trans-Siberian Railway had been completed, helping the development of Russian influence in the Far East. The industrial growth was concentrated in St Petersburg, Moscow, Baku and Ukraine, with much of it centred in relatively large factories. By 1900 over half of the industrial workforce was employed in factories with more than a thousand workers. As a result, large cities grew at a phenomenal rate. The population of St Petersburg, for example, doubled between 1890 and 1914, from 1 million to 2 million.

> **Take note**
> What were the main effects of Witte's economic reforms?

This successful economic development allowed Russia to exploit the vast natural resources of Siberia. It also allowed Russia to develop its military power, because the capital goods developed in this period were also used for military production.

The rapid growth of towns and cities inevitably led to the creation of poor living and working conditions. And this provided the ideal environment for the development of social unrest and support for radical alternatives to Tsarism. Many of the new industrial workers became disillusioned with what they found. In St Petersburg, for example, workers at the Putilov engineering works – which employed thousands – had become sufficiently disillusioned by 1905 to demonstrate and strike for better conditions. Their actions provided the beginning of the 1905 Revolution.

For all the economic improvement under Witte, Russia still lagged behind the other Great Powers in economic growth over the period from 1890 to 1914. In addition, the extra taxation placed on the peasantry caused deep resentment, and by the first five years of the twentieth century, peasant uprisings were becoming commonplace.

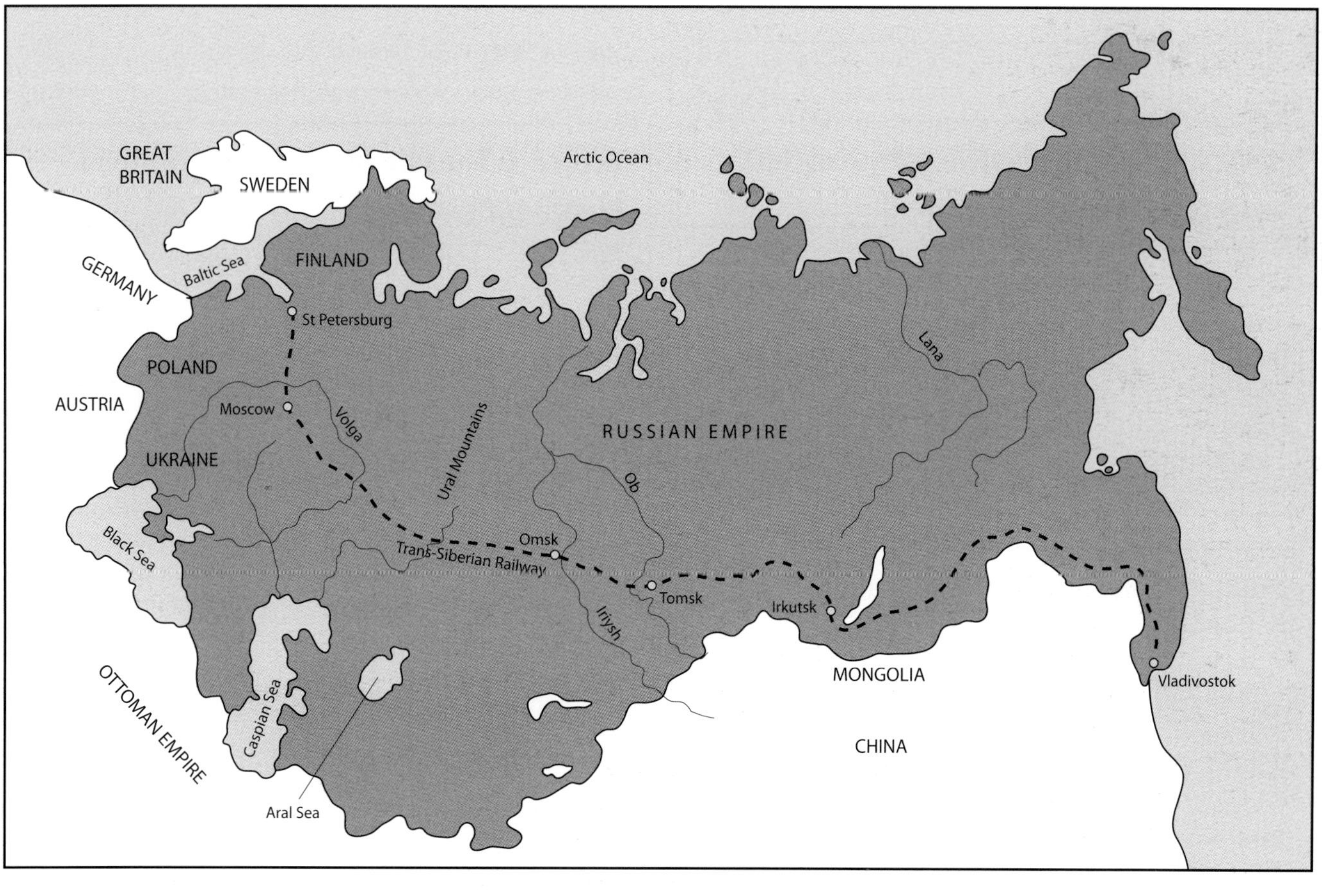

The Trans-Siberian Railway

Activity: Rapid industrialisation

What were the main advantages and disadvantages of the period of rapid industrialisation under Witte?

Activity: Were Witte's policies successful? Interpreting the economic data

Sources 1–5 below show various data about the Russian economy.

1. Can you identify any data to support the view that Witte's aim to industrialise the Russian economy was a success? (Remember Witte was Finance Minister from 1893 to 1903.) Mention precise data in support of your view.
2. Did Witte achieve his aim of helping Russia catch up with its Great Power rivals? Identify the relevant sources and mention precise data in support of your view.

Source 1: The development of the Russian railway network

Date	*Km constructed*
1881	21,228
1891	31,219
1900	53,234
1914	70,156

Source 2: The rate of economic growth

Date	*Increases in millions of tonnes*			
	Coal	*Iron*	*Oil*	*Cereals**
1880	3.2	0.4	0.5	34
1890	5.9	0.9	3.9	36
1900	16.1	2.7	10.2	56
1910	26.8	3.7	9.7	74

*Cereals figure is for European Russia only.

Source 3: The comparative growth of the economies of the Great Powers

	Increase in national income, 1894–1913
Austria–Hungary	79%
Britain	70%
Germany	58%
France	52%
European Russia	50%

Source 4: The rate of industrial growth in Russia 1885–1913

Period	*Annual average growth rate*
1885–89	6.1%
1890–09	8.0%
1900–06	1.4%
1907–13	6.2%

Source 5: The growth of towns and cities

	Population in thousands		
	1863	*1897*	*1914*
St Petersburg	539	1300	2100
Moscow	462	1030	1700
Kiev	68	247	520
Odessa*	119	403	499
Baku**	14	12	211

* The major grain-exporting port

** The centre of oil production

Source of data: M. Falkus, *The Industrialisation of Russia,* Macmillan, 1972

Chapter 4 Radical parties

Key questions

- Why were radical parties formed in late Tsarist Russia?
- How did they grow and develop?
- What impact did they have on Russian politics?

Before the 1905 Revolution, the Tsar had complete political authority within Russia – no political parties were permitted. Therefore, the many radical political parties and groupings that were formed were illegal. They all had one thing in common – they wanted to see an end to the Tsarist autocracy. But that was the only aim they had in common. Radical parties covered the entire political spectrum – from moderate liberals to extremists who advocated the use of violence to overthrow the Tsar. Radical parties also included nationalists, such as Poles, who wanted to separate from the Russian Empire. How did these radical parties come into being and what impact did they have on Russia in the years before the First World War?

The tradition of radicalism

The forerunner of radical parties within Russia was the Populist (Narodnik) movement of the 1860s and 1870s. Following the emancipation of the serfs, in 1861, Populists looked to Russia's peasants as the political basis of future society. Populists disliked the autocratic rule of Tsars and wanted to replace it with a system of government based on independent peasant communes, a form of very local democracy. They also believed that in this new peasant society the strong central government would fade way. This was a unique Russian way to change society and it was influenced greatly by a Russian exile, Alexander Herzen, who disliked the development of western society that he witnessed in Paris and London. He spread his ideas within Russia through a periodical called

The Socialist Revolutionary (SR) Party

Like the Populists, the Socialist Revolutionaries believed Russia's future lay with the peasantry. They were led by Victor Chernov, a member of the educated middle class, who attempted to broaden the appeal of his party by winning support from the growing number of industrial workers. To him, Russia's future lay with 'the people' and the people were a combination of peasants and workers – the discontented elements of Russian society. The SR promised that all peasants would be given their own land, without compensating the previous owners. But the party was never a strongly knit group, more a wide variety of factions. At one extreme were anarchists who disliked central political authority and were attracted by the SR's plan for independent peasant communes. The party also contained a terrorist wing, similar to the 'People's Will', which between 1901 and 1905 was responsible for a wave of political assassinations, including Plehve, the Minister of the Interior, in 1904 and the Tsar's uncle, Grand Duke Sergei, during the early months of the 1905 Revolution. On the left of the party was a group which supported peasant socialism, a radical idea not too dissimilar from the socialist ideas of the Social Democrats. In October 1917, the 'Left SRs' joined with the Bolshevik faction of the Social Democrats to form the world's first Communist government.

Social Revolutionaries played an important role in the 1905 Revolution with their support for peasant uprisings. At the height of the Revolution the 'All-Russian Union of Peasants' was created which became an SR stronghold. At its first Congress in 1906 it again called for peasant ownership of land. This was its most popular policy by far and one which made the SRs the largest radical party in Russia before 1917.

The Social Democrat Party

Although the SRs were large in number, the creation of the Social Democrat Party in Minsk in 1898 was of greater significance to the future of Russia. The SRs looked towards a unique Russian way of political development, but the Social Democrats looked west – to the radical ideas of Marxism.

For Marxism to succeed in Russia, industrial development was essential. During Witte's 'Great Spurt' Russia was becoming an industrial state but still had a vast population of peasants. To the Social Democrats, Witte's policies would hasten the day when Russia was ripe for socialist revolution. But in 1898 Russia was still far from having a majority population of industrial workers. So how could socialist revolution be possible under such social and economic conditions?

The split between Mensheviks and Bolsheviks

A leading Social Democrat who addressed the question of how the party differed from the SRs was Vladimir Ilyich Ulyanov, better known as Lenin. In 1902 he published the pamphlet, *What is to be Done?*, in which he outlined his plan for the creation of a radical party of political revolutionaries who would lead Russia in socialist revolution. To Marx, historical development could be studied scientifically and predicted through his model of social and

Take note

In what ways was the Socialist Revolutionary Party similar to the Populist movement?

Viktor Chernov

(1873–1952)

A leading member of the Socialist Revolutionary Party. He attended Moscow University, and in the early 1890s joined the Populist movement. After spending some time organising the peasants within Russia he went to Switzerland in 1899. He joined the newly-founded Social Revolutionary Party and became the editor of its newspaper *Revolutionary Russia.* He returned to Russia after the Revolution of 1905, was elected to the Second Duma and became a leader of the SR faction. In 1917, Chernov was the Minister for Agriculture in the Provisional Government. He was also the last Chairman of the Russian Constituent Assembly in January 1918. During the Russian Civil War (1918–1921) he fled to Western Europe and then the United States.

Take note

1. In what ways was the Social Democrat Party different from the Social Revolutionary Party, in its aims and methods?
2. Give reasons for the split of the Social Democrat Party into two major factions from 1903.

Marx's view of political and economic development

The basis of Marx's ideas were laid out in *The Communist Manifesto*, which he and Friedrich Engels published in 1848.To Marx, society was made up of competing social and economic classes. Whichever class held economic power (or controlled the means of production) also held political power. Marx believed that conflict between these different classes was the basis of historical development and, as a result, history went through a number of distinct phases in which these classes clashed, producing a new social and economic system each time. Marx believed that this historical process was inevitable.

The key phases in Marx's view of history were as follows:

Feudal phase

Competing social and economic classes: Landowners and serfs/peasants

This will change when society industrialises and the business middle class (e.g. factory owners) gain more power, leading to...

Capitalist phase

Competing social and economic classes: Business middle class (bourgeoisie) and industrial workers (proletariat)

This will change when industrial workers are treated so badly under capitalism that they will start a revolution and take control of the means of production, leading to...

Socialist phase

In the socialist phase, equality and harmony will develop under the political guidance of the industrial working class.

This will change when all class conflict finally ends, leading to a new, ideal state called...

Communism

To Marx, the beginning of the end of the Feudal phase was the French Revolution of 1789. This began the Bourgeois/Capitalist phase, which was associated with industrialisation and the creation of an industrial working class – the 'proletariat'.

economic conflict. Lenin saw politics in a very similar way. Revolution had to be organised and planned scientifically – and Lenin was a very determined man.

The Second Party Congress of the Social Democratic Party was held in 1903. It took place in London because for much of its existence the Social Democrat leadership was forced to live abroad to avoid arrest by the Okhrana. At the Congress, the party split into two major factions. The main culprit for the split was Lenin, who demanded that the Social Democrats should limit their membership to those dedicated revolutionaries who would lead a workers' revolution. The Mensheviks opposed this idea. They wanted the Social Democrats to have a broad membership, admitting anyone who was in sympathy with the party's aims. Despite an initial defeat for Lenin's idea by 28 votes to 22, he eventually ensured that the Congress accepted his view. This occurred after the Jewish Bund faction had left the Congress. When Lenin's idea was raised again, he won by 17 votes to 15. Because Lenin won this final vote, his followers were known as Bolsheviks (the majority), and his opponents were known as Mensheviks (the minority). In reality, however, the Mensheviks outnumbered the Bolsheviks.

Lenin's contribution to the development of Russian Marxism was not limited to party organisation. He also developed the idea that the class struggle within Russia was not limited to businessmen and industrial workers. He

Karl Marx

(1818–1883)

A German political philosopher and founder of Marxism. He worked closely with a German factory owner, Friedrich Engels, in developing his views on history , economics and society. In 1848, in Brussels, they produced *The Communist Manifesto* which stated that history was based on class struggle between competing social and economic groups. The society most likely to experience communist revolution was one that had experienced an industrial revolution. To Marx, the country least likely to experience this type of revolution was Russia, which was overwhelmingly agricultural.

Glossary:

Jewish Bund

Popular name for the General Jewish Labour Union – a Jewish political faction within the Social Democrat Party. It wanted a socialist Russia where anti-Semitic discrimination was abolished.

Franchise

The right to vote.

saw conflict in the Russian countryside too, between rich peasants (known as Kulaks) and poorer peasants. Later, when Communist Russia was created under Lenin's leadership, it became a Socialist republic of industrial workers and poor peasants.

Take note

1. In what ways were the Liberals and Social Democrats similar?
2. Why was the 1905 Revolution an important turning point in the development of Russian liberalism?
3. Does the Octobrists' programme show that they were a radical party?

The development of Russian liberalism

Within Russia, Western European liberalism was an idea which was associated with the educated middle class. This group included administrative officials and university-educated professionals such as lawyers, doctors and teachers. Liberalism in Russia comprised different groups at different times.

Zemstva

The beginnings of liberalism within Russia can be traced back to the creation of the zemstva during the reign of Alexander II. Zemstva were the first political organisations in Russian history which contained elected officials. By the end of the nineteenth century, attempts were made to create a national organisation for the zemstva. The leading political figure behind this move was D. Shipov, the chairman of the Moscow zemstvo. In 1899 Shipov was able to persuade the Interior Minister to create zemstva across western Russia.

Union of Liberation

In 1901, some Russian liberal exiles in Germany established a newspaper called *Liberation*, supporting the idea of a constitutional monarchy, similar to Britain, with an elected national parliament based on a democratic franchise. In 1904 these liberal exiles formed the 'Union of Liberation'.

Octobrists

The 1905 Revolution had a profound effect on the development of Russian liberalism. A turning point came when the Tsar issued the October Manifesto

The Octobrists' programme, created after the 1905 October Manifesto

The Octobrists saw their main task as being to help bring about the rapid establishment of a constitutional monarchy, on the basis of the manifesto of 17 October, and to the rapid convocation of the State Duma (parliament). The Octobrists wanted change, but they rejected revolution and called for law and order to be restored. They wanted a strong and authoritative regime, but one that would work with the representatives of the people in the Duma to bring peace and stability to Russia through constructive legislation.

The basis of the Octobrists' programme was:

1. The preservation of the unity of the Russian state.
2. The development and strengthening of the foundations of a constitutional monarchy with a representative assembly elected on a broad franchise.
3. The guaranteeing of civil rights.
4. The urgent summoning of the State Duma, to put through political reforms to deal with such matters as:
   (a) the peasant question – the peasantry should be granted the same civil rights as the rest of the population; peasant land-holding should be extended and regulated.
   (b) workers' insurance, a limitation of the working day and the freedom to form trade unions and to strike.
   (c) the development of local self-government.
   (d) measures on education.
   (e) judicial and administrative reforms.
   (f) economic and financial measures to achieve a more rational and just tax system.

because, for the first time in Russian history, the Tsar was willing to share political power in national government. The Manifesto suggested that a national parliament be created which, to many Russian liberals, was a crucial breakthrough. This group became known as the Union of October 17 or simply the 'Octobrists'. They believed that the October Manifesto provided the best settlement for Russia's constitutional development, and from 1905 they were supporters of Tsar Nicholas II.

Kadets

A more radical liberal group which came out of the 1905 Revolution were the Constitutional Democrats (Kadets). They saw the October Manifesto as the beginning, not the end, of political reform. They hoped that a truly parliamentary system of government, based on a democratic franchise, would be the best way to deal with the social and economic problems facing Russia in the early years of the twentieth century.

The Constitutional Democratic (Kadet) Party's programme, 1905

Basic rights of citizens

1. All Russian citizens, irrespective of sex, religion or nationality, are equal before the law. All class distinctions and all limitations of personal and property rights of Poles, Jews, and all other groups of the population, should be repealed.
2. Every citizen is guaranteed freedom of religion.
3. Freedom of the Press.
4. Right to organise public or private meetings and to organise unions or societies without needing permission.

Government apparatus

5. The constitutional system of the Russian state will be determined by the constitution.
6. Elections by a secret ballot, irrespective of voters' religion, nationality or sex.
7. No ukase (imperial decree) by the Tsar without the support of the national parliament.
8. Local self-government should be extended throughout the entire Russian Empire.

Yuli Martov

(1873–1923)

Born Yuly Tsederbaum. Originally a member of the Jewish Bund of socialists, he was a close friend of Lenin, assisting him in the publication of the socialist newspaper *Iskra* (The Spark) which was produced in London and smuggled into Russia in the early years of the twentieth century.

He opposed Lenin's ideas on party membership at the Second Party Congress of 1903 and subsequently led the Menshevik faction. After the 1905 Revolution, Martov argued that revolutionaries should join forces with trade unions, cooperatives and village communes to oppose the government and help bring about the economic and social conditions that would make it possible for a socialist revolution to take place. He supported the reunification with the Bolsheviks in the 1905 Revolution but the factions separated again in 1907 and split permanently in 1912.

Radical parties and groups in Russia

The Social Democrats (Russian Social Democratic Labour Party (RSDLP))

- Social Democrats took their inspiration from Western ideas about the development of society.
- They were Marxists who aimed to overthrow the Tsar and establish a socialist society.
- The Social Democrats were willing to use peaceful and violent means to achieve their aims.
- At the Second Party Congress in London in 1903 the party split into two major factions – the Bolsheviks, who supported Lenin, and the Mensheviks led by Yuli Martov. There were other groups, such as the Jewish Bund and the Inter-District Group, which had Trotsky as a member.
- Bolsheviks became known as Communists from 1918.

Socialist Revolutionaries (SRs)

- The SRs took their inspiration from a Russian view on how to develop society.
- This radical party wanted to redistribute all land to the Russian peasantry. Unsurprisingly, as peasants comprised 80 per cent of the population, it became the most widely supported party in Russia.
- SRs were willing to use peaceful and violent means to achieve theirs aims.

The Liberals

- The Liberals were members of the middle class who wanted more political freedom in Russia. They wished to see Russia develop along the lines of Western states with parliamentary governments, such as Britain.
- Liberals were only prepared to use peaceful means to achieve their aims.
- From 1905 they were divided into two main groups – Octobrists, who regarded the October Manifesto of 1905 as the basis of the Russian political system and the limit of constitutional change, and the Constitutional Democrats (Kadets) who saw the October Manifesto as the first step towards full parliamentary government in Russia.

Activity: The Octobrists and the Kadets

Study the programmes of the Octobrists and the Kadets. Can you identify any similarities and differences between them?

Activity: Radical parties in Russia

Using information contained within this chapter, fill in the table below.

When you have completed the table, answer the following questions:

1. Which party do you regard as the most radical? Give reasons for your answer.
2. Can you identify any similarities between the parties?
3. Which radical party do you think was most likely to succeed in its aims in the years before 1914?

	Aims	Support	Methods	How radical?
Social Democrats (Bolsheviks)				
Social Democrats (Mensheviks)				
Social Revolutionaries				
Liberals (Octobrists)				
Liberals (Kadets)				

Chapter 5 1905 – a failed revolution?

Key questions

- Why did revolution break out in Russia in 1905?
- How did the Revolution develop during 1905?
- What were the consequences of the Revolution?

On Sunday 9 January 1905, a large crowd of 150,000 workers demonstrated outside the Tsar's Winter Palace in the Russian capital, St Petersburg. In what was a peaceful demonstration, the workers wished to present a petition to the Tsar. The petition asked for reforms, such as an end to the Russo-Japanese War, expanded suffrage, an 8-hour working day, higher pay and the end to forced overtime in factories. They were led by Father Gapon, a Russian Orthodox priest, who was also a double agent for the Okhrana. Unfortunately, the Tsar was not in the Winter Palace that day, but this did not stop the police from fearing trouble. Troops were used to disperse the demonstration and in the process almost a thousand demonstrators were killed. The event was known as 'Bloody Sunday'. It helped spark a revolution across Russia which lasted for a year. During that time the country faced peasant uprisings, strikes and demands for political reform. It seemed that the Tsar himself might be forced from power. So why did Russia descend into a year of revolutionary turmoil?

'The 1905 Revolution did more than anything else during Nicholas II's reign to undermine support for the regime.'

Richard Charques, historian

What were the long-term causes of the 1905 Revolution?

Unlike the later Bolshevik Revolution of October 1917, the 1905 Revolution was spontaneous. It was not planned, but took place as a result of considerable resentment about the social, economic and political situation in Russia. Bloody Sunday unleashed a wave of unrest and violence that had been gradually building up within Russia for several years.

Social and economic causes

Before 1905 the vast majority (80 per cent) of the Russian population was made up of peasants – agricultural labourers – with most living in poverty. To make matters worse, the Russian population was growing rapidly – from 98 million in 1885 to 125 million by 1905. The size of peasant landholdings fell in an attempt to provide individual plots for each peasant family. Even though they lived in poverty, peasants were able to survive as long as the harvests were good. But in 1892, 1898 and 1901 there were harvest failures,

Russian calendar

Before 1918, Russia used the Julian calendar, which was thirteen days behind the Gregorian calendar used by the rest of Europe. When Bloody Sunday occurred, therefore, it was 9 January in Russia, but 22 January in the rest of Europe. This book uses the Russian dates.

Glossary: Double agent

A person who acts as a spy for two opposing sides.

Take note

1. Identify the social and economic causes of the 1905 Revolution.
2. Identify the political reasons why the Revolution occurred.

which caused widespread famine. Peasants reacted with violence. In what were known as jacqueries, peasants attacked government officials and destroyed government records on landholdings – especially those documents which referred to unpaid rents on land. By 1905 the Russian countryside seemed on the verge of revolution.

While Russian agriculture remained backward compared to the rest of Europe, the rest of the Russian economy went through a period of spectacular growth in the fifteen years before 1905. Under the leadership of Finance Minister, Witte, Russia began to industrialise rapidly. This led to the rapid growth of population in towns and cities as peasants moved from the land to find jobs in factories. By 1905 cities like St Petersburg and Moscow had slums full of former peasants who had become industrial workers. Their working and living conditions were extremely poor, and it was this group who demonstrated outside the Winter Palace on Bloody Sunday.

So a major cause of resentment against the Tsar's regime was social and economic in origin. Both in industry and in agriculture, Russian peasants and workers faced the uncertainty of poverty and poor living conditions. As a result, demands for political change had a willing audience.

Political causes

In January 1905 Russia was still an autocracy, with the Tsar possessing complete political power. Unlike other major European states, Russia did not have an elected national parliament, the only elected bodies being the zemstva. By 1905 the demand for political reform was growing, but the reformers were a mixed group with little in common – other than their opposition to the Tsarist autocracy. The most moderate reformers were liberals – lawyers and other professionals – who wanted the Tsar to share political power with a parliament elected by the more wealthy members of the population.

A more extreme group was the Social Revolutionaries. Founded in 1901, this group wanted to give political power to the peasants, and were willing to use violence to achieve their aims. In the years 1901 to 1905 they were responsible for over two thousand assassinations which included the Interior Minister, Plehve in 1904 and the Tsar's uncle, Grand Duke Sergei, the governor-general of Moscow, who was assassinated on 4 February 1905.

The most extreme radical group was the Social Democrats who were also willing to use violent revolution to achieve their aims. Founded in 1898, this group wanted to create a completely new type of society which gave power to workers and peasants. In 1905 it split into two groups – Bolsheviks and Mensheviks. However, most of its leaders were in prison or in exile. Once Bloody Sunday had occurred, many of the exiled reformers returned to Russia in an attempt to use the widespread unrest to force political change.

What were the immediate causes of the 1905 revolution?

The Russo–Japanese War

An important event which undermined support for the Tsar's regime was the Russo-Japanese War. Like other Great Powers, Russia aimed to expand its empire in the late nineteenth century. While countries like Britain and France concentrated on Africa, Russia attempted to expand its control over the Far East. In doing so, it came into direct conflict with another expansionist power, Japan. From 1904 to 1905 Russia and Japan went to war over control of northern China and Korea. Although the Russians saw themselves as far superior in military power, they suffered a humiliating defeat. In January 1905 the Russians were forced to surrender their Port Arthur naval base in north China, and in the following months Japanese forces defeated the Russian army in Manchuria.

Russian defeats were seen as national humiliation and helped cause unrest against the government. The greatest military humiliation of all took place on 27 May 1905 at the Battle of Tsushima. The Russian Baltic fleet had sailed almost halfway round the world – from northern Europe to the Far East – only to lose 25 out of its 35 warships in a crushing defeat by the Japanese navy. Russia's humiliation in the Russo-Japanese War undermined support for the Tsar. It also helped prolong the Revolution as many of the events of the war took place after the Revolution had begun. Further defeats during 1905 made the government and Tsar look even weaker and gave encouragement to the revolutionaries.

Bloody Sunday

Bloody Sunday was a disaster for the government and the Tsar. The demonstration had been peaceful and was led by a priest, leading to

Tsarist troops fire on demonstrators in front of the Winter Palace, Bloody Sunday, January 1905

Father George Gapon

(1870–1906)

The son of a wealthy farmer, Gapon became a priest after being widowed in 1898. He then moved to St Petersburg, where he preached in workers' districts and ran into trouble with the Church authorities over his drinking and gambling. He organised the Assembly of Russian Factory and Mill Workers of St Petersburg, which existed to defend workers' rights and to improve their religious status. The Assembly was secretly supported by the Okhrana in an attempt to get information on factory worker activity and, ultimately to control the Assembly and keep out the revolutionaries. Soon the organisation had twelve branches and 8,000 members and from 1904, the Assembly became more radical. Following Bloody Sunday, Gapon called upon workers to take action against the regime, but soon after he escaped abroad, where he fell in with the Socialist Revolutionaries. Gapon returned to Russian later in 1905 after the October Manifesto, and resumed his work with the Okhrana. Suspected as a double agent, Gapon was hanged in 1906, in a cottage in Finland, in accordance with a sentence passed on him by the Socialist Revolutionary Party.

widespread outrage from many sections of society, not just revolutionaries and radicals. After Bloody Sunday, many of the surviving demonstrators were expelled from St Petersburg. This only served to spread the news of the massacre further and spark sympathy strikes in other parts of the Russian empire. It also seriously damaged the Tsar's popularity: prior to 1905 many ordinary Russians thought of the Tsar as a 'Little Father' who was fundamentally on their side and who would listen if they petitioned him. Bloody Sunday destroyed this trust.

How did the Revolution develop during 1905?

Revolutionary activity took many forms. As it was an unplanned revolution it comprised a variety of protests by workers, peasants and members of the armed forces. The lack of coordination ultimately led to the failure of the Revolution. However, it also caused problems for the government, which did not know when and where the next threat to its authority would appear.

Strikes

One important aspect of the Revolution was the outbreak of strikes by industrial workers. In February 1905, some 400,000 workers went on strike in response to Bloody Sunday, and by the end of 1905 over 2.7 million workers had been on strike. The wave of strikes by the workers developed into a general strike from 20 September to 30 October 1905. The strikers were organised by the discontented workers themselves and not by the revolutionaries (who were taken by surprise by the swift spread of the strikes). The workers and peasants had developed some organising abilities through their strikes and riots before 1905. Strikers set up soviets (workers' councils) to direct the strikes – first in St Petersburg, then in Moscow and other industrial centres. This was the first, greatest, most thoroughly carried out and most successful general strike in Russian history. The whole country was paralysed. When the railway workers went on strike in October, the government was seriously threatened. In a country as large as Russia, the railways were crucial for the movement of troops to put down unrest away from the cities.

Peasant uprisings (jacqueries)

Faced with poor harvests and high taxes, peasants rose in revolt across Russia. The first major uprising occurred in February 1905 in Kursk province, and by the end of the year most of European Russia had been affected by outbreaks of peasant unrest.

Mutinies

The key to the success or failure of the Revolution was the armed forces. After Bloody Sunday, mutinies occurred in some army units and parts of the navy. The most famous mutiny occurred in the Black Sea fleet in June 1905, when the crew of the battleship

Tsar's authority. However, at no time during the 1905 Revolution was the army likely to turn against the regime.

The St Petersburg Soviet

An important feature of the Revolution was the creation of an assembly of workers, the St Petersburg Soviet. It was a product of a general strike in the capital which began in October 1905. Groups of workers from the capital elected representatives to the Soviet, and at its height it had over 400 members, representing 96 factories. One of the leading figures was the Social Democrat, Leon Trotsky. Although the Soviet published demands for radical social reform, most of its work was trying to organise strikes and ensuring that striking workers received food. The most important radical group linked to the Soviet was the Mensheviks, with the Bolsheviks forming a minority. But the Soviet came to an end on 3 December, when government troops arrested its leaders. Although the St Petersburg Soviet was closed down, its very existence (along with similar Soviets in other towns and cities) showed that the workers were capable of organising themselves and challenging the government in a co-ordinated way.

Armed uprising

The strikes continued through the late autumn and early winter of 1905, with many turning violent. On 5 December a general strike took place in Moscow, but by 7 December it had become an armed uprising. During the next nine days several thousand armed workers waged a violent struggle with the police and government troops. By 18 December, with around a thousand people dead and parts of the city in ruins, the revolutionaries, including many Bolsheviks, surrendered. The Revolution was over.

Timeline

1905	
January	Bloody Sunday
	Port Arthur surrenders to the Japanese
February	Assassination of Grand Duke Sergei, the Tsar's uncle
	Major strike involving 400,000 workers
April	Peasant uprising begins in Kursk province
May	Battle of Tsushima
June	Mutiny on the battleship *Potemkin*
October	Railway workers strike
	Creation of St Petersburg Soviet
	October Manifesto
1906	
April	First Duma meets in Tauride Palace, St Petersburg

The government reaction

By the autumn of 1905 Russia had suffered strikes, peasant uprisings and mutinies in the armed forces. It seemed that unless something was done the Tsar might be forced from power. On 30 October, 1905 the Tsar's government acted. It issued a proclamation, the October Manifesto. This Manifesto promised reforms. In particular, it accepted the proposal that an elected national Parliament be created. It also proposed freedom of speech, religion and civil rights. These proposals pleased liberals, and many liberals accepted the Manifesto as an important but final reform. These liberals became known as Octobrists. Other liberals, known as the Kadets, saw the October Manifesto as the beginning of a new era of reform. However, more radical groups such as Mensheviks, Bolsheviks and SRs wanted major social and economic reform as well. As a result, the October Manifesto split the revolutionaries.

Issuing the October Manifesto was a major turning point in the 1905 Revolution. It began the process whereby the Tsar regained control.

Take note

Identify at least three reasons why you think the 1905 Revolution failed to overthrow the Tsar.

Why did the Revolution come to an end?

> **Take note**
>
> Using the information below (a) list the differences between Party and government, and (b) list the ways in which the Communist Party increasingly took control of the government.

The loyalty of the armed forces

Although there were some mutinies, the majority of armed forces stayed loyal to the Tsar. As a result, the disturbances, which were part of the Revolution, were crushed and the army arrested thousands of revolutionaries. Many were executed, and thousands more were exiled in Siberia. Most of the leaders who were left, including Trotsky and Lenin, fled the country.

In October 1905 the government began to reassert its authority. It supported the formation of a new political group, the 'Union of Russian People', which was linked to pro-government terrorist groups called the Black Hundreds. These counter-revolutionary groups helped the government regain control of the country, with the Black Hundreds hunting down and 'executing' thousands of known reformers.

> **Take note**
>
> To what extent can the events of 1905 in Russia be regarded as a 'revolution'?

The lack of unity among the revolutionaries

One of the reasons for the Revolution's failure was the lack of central coordination. The spontaneity of the revolutionary outbreaks meant that the armed forces, the police and the Black Hundreds could suppress them, one by one. At no time was the government threatened by wholesale, coordinated revolutionary activity. Although the St Petersburg Soviet organised strikes it had very little power over the strikers and in late 1905 it was closed down and its leaders arrested.

Another aspect of the lack of unity was the fact that the revolutionaries had very different aims. The liberals, who were never one political group, wanted to share power with the Tsar. The Social Revolutionaries wanted peasant ownership of land. The Social Democrats, who were divided between Bolsheviks and Mensheviks, wanted to completely change society and remove the Tsar. As a result, on many occasions the different radical groups fought amongst themselves as much as opposing the government.

Splitting the opposition

The October Manifesto split the opposition to the government. Unlike the liberals, the more extreme revolutionaries, such as the Social Revolutionaries and the Social Democrats rejected the Manifesto outright and continued their opposition to the government.

The Manifesto was the turning point in the Revolution. From then on, the Tsar's government regained control. Although disturbances continued into 1906, the Revolution had failed to topple the Tsar and his government.

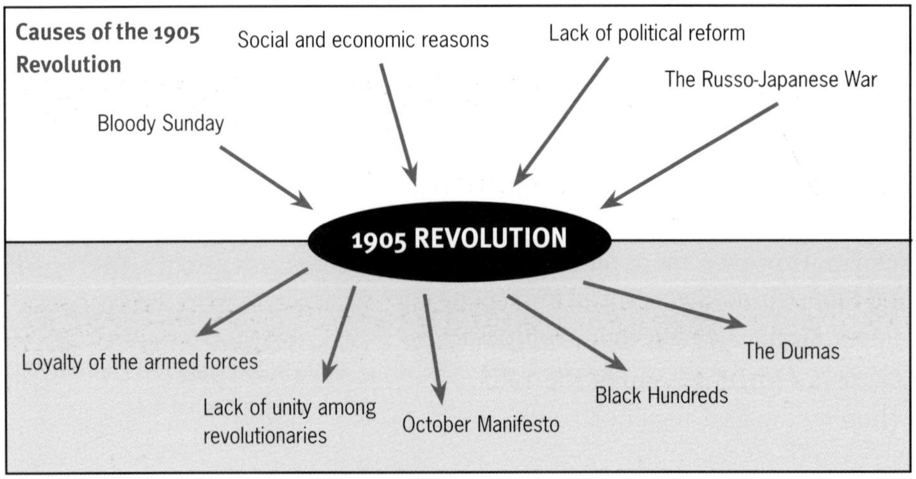

Reasons for the failure of the 1905 revolution

The consequences of the 1905 Revolution

The Fundamental Law 1906

The Tsar survived the Revolution, and in 1906 he issued the 'Fundamental Law'. This became the constitution of the Russian Empire, creating a national parliament, with the Lower House – the Duma – being elected. The Upper House – the Council of State – was partly elected and partly nominated by the Tsar. Article 87 of the Fundamental Law gave the right to the Tsar to govern by decree, thereby ignoring parliament. And the Tsar still kept the right to choose his own government. So the Tsar still retained considerable political power, and his changes fell far short of the demands of most of the revolutionaries.

The Dumas

The first Duma was elected in April 1906. It contained large numbers of deputies who wanted major reform, such as land reform and release of political prisoners. The Duma lasted only 73 days before the Tsar dissolved it, using his powers under the Fundamental Law. A second Duma was elected in February 1907, but it also contained many reformers – much to the displeasure of the Tsar and his chief minister, Peter Stolypin. As a result, it was replaced by a third Duma in November 1907. This time there was a much more restricted franchise. Now only the wealthy could vote – which excluded most of the reformers' supporters. Not surprisingly, the election produced a majority sympathetic to the Tsar, and from 1907 to 1912 he faced little demand for reform from Russia's first national parliament.

Activity: The Russo-Japanese War

Do you think that 'Russian defeat in the Russo-Japanese War was a cause of the Revolution' or that ' Defeat made the Revolution worse once it had begun'? Give reasons for your answer.

Activity: The outbreak of Revolution

What do you regard as the most important reason for the outbreak of Revolution in 1905? Give reasons for your answer.

Activity: Reasons for failure

Place the reasons for the failure of the 1905 Revolution in order of importance. Write a sentence next to each reason explaining its importance.

Activity: Successes and failures

What do you regard as the main successes and main failures of the 1905 Revolution?

Skills Builder 1: **Writing in paragraphs**

In the examination you will have to write an essay-style answer on Russia in Revolution, in approximately 40 minutes. When producing an essay-style answer, it is important that you write in paragraphs. You will need to make a number of points to build up your argument so that it answers the question you have been asked. You should write a paragraph to address each point.

What should you include in a paragraph?

In a paragraph you should:

- Make a point to support your argument and answer the question.
- Provide evidence to support your point.
- Explain how your evidence supports your point.
- Explain how your points relate to the essay question.

Remember: POINT – EVIDENCE – EXPLANATION

It is important that you construct your answer this way. If you just 'tell a story' in which you produce factual knowledge without explanation in relation to the question, you will not get high marks.

An example

Here is an example of a question asking you to produce not a story, but an explanation:

(A) Explain why the 1905 Revolution failed.

The information to answer this question can be found in Chapter 5. The reasons you could include are:

- The continued loyalty of the armed forces
- The disunity among the revolutionaries
- The October Manifesto
- The use of the Black Hundreds.

As you plan, it is important to form your ideas about the *significance* of these reasons. Remember that, whichever one you decide was the most important, you need to convince the examiner that your chosen reason was the key one.

Here is an example of a paragraph which could form part of your answer:

The most important reason why the 1905 Revolution failed was the loyalty of the armed forces to the Tsar and his government. Even though there were some minor mutinies, such as the battleship *Potemkin* in the Black Sea, the armed forces helped crush the Revolution. An example was the suppression of the Moscow Revolt of December 1905. The revolutionaries lacked weapons and military training so, unless the armed forces deserted the Tsar, the Revolution had no chance of success.

This is a good paragraph because:

- It begins with a clear statement which focuses on a reason for failure.
- It *prioritises* reasons by stating, in the opening sentence that this was the key reason.
- The opening statement is backed up by evidence. It points out the role of the armed forces in defeating the Revolution.
- The final sentence links the role of the armed forces clearly with the defeat of the revolutionaries.

Activity: Write your own paragraph

Now try writing a paragraph on one of the other reasons for the failure of the 1905 Revolution. The information you require is in Chapter 5.

Remember to begin your paragraph with *why* you think the point is important. Make sure that you support your answer with factual knowledge and evidence. Then round off your paragraph by explaining how what it says links back to the question.

You may find the following steps a useful guide:

1. First decide what point you are going to make. Make sure that the point is relevant to the question you have been asked. For example:
   - Because the revolutionaries were divided in their aims, they could not unite to overthrow the Tsar.
   - The revolutionaries in the 1905 revolution were not organised or coordinated enough to overthrow the Tsar, and this was the main reason why the Revolution failed.
   - Although disunity among the revolutionaries did not help the Revolution, this was not the main reason for its failure.

(You may wish to argue a different point of your own.)

2. Decide which evidence you will use to support your point. But choose carefully – make sure that it is relevant and is linked directly to the point you are making.
3. Write your paragraph by:
   - Presenting your point
   - Backing your point up with evidence
   - Explaining how the evidence supports your point
   - Explaining how your point relates to the essay question.

Remember: POINT – EVIDENCE – EXPLANATION

Extension work

Here is an example of the style of question often used in the examination. It asks you to make a judgement about causes:

(B) How far was the Russo-Japanese War of 1904–1905 responsible for the outbreak of the 1905 Revolution?

If you were writing an essay-style answer on this question, you would be expected to select information which helps explain why the 1905 Revolution occurred and to decide on the importance of the Russo-Japanese War compared with other factors that were causing opposition and discontent in Russia at the time. Using the steps above to help you, write a paragraph to form part of an essay on the question.

Chapter 6 Stolypin – repression and reform

Key questions

- How effective was repression under Stolypin?
- Why did Stolypin embark on social and economic reform?
- Were the Dumas a success or a failure?

The 1905 Revolution had almost toppled the Tsarist regime. The Tsar had survived – but for how long? In the aftermath of the Revolution it fell upon the Tsar's chief minister, Peter Stolypin, to bring stability and re-establish political control. The period after the 1905 Revolution was one of ruthless political repression. So great was the use of executions that the nooses used in hangings became known as 'Stolypin's neckties'. However, Stolypin was no mere reactionary. Not only did he repress political opponents, but he also tried to bring social and economic stability to the regime in order to prevent any future outbreak of revolution. This period saw Russia entering a new era where, for the first time, the country had an elected national parliament, the Duma. Was this a major step towards parliamentary government or was it merely 'window dressing' for the continuation of Tsarist autocracy?

Take note

What actions did Stolypin take to restore order in Russia after the 1905 Revolution?

The failure of the 1905 Revolution was accompanied by severe and ruthless political repression. October 1905 was a month of both reform and repression. On the one hand, the Tsar issued the October Manifesto. But on the other, the government supported the creation of the 'Union of the Russian People', a political party designed to defend the Tsarist regime, with links to the terrorist gangs known as the Black Hundreds. The Black Hundreds attacked thousands of known or suspected reformers, with Jews being singled out for specific punishment in co-ordinated and violent attacks known as 'pogroms'.

In November 1905 government forces closed down the St Petersburg Soviet and the All-Russia Union of Peasants, arresting the members. The final act of Revolution, an uprising in Moscow in December 1905, was ruthlessly crushed by the army, with around a thousand rebels killed and hundreds arrested and imprisoned.

In the aftermath of the Revolution, repression became associated with one man, Peter Stolypin. He had joined the Council of Ministers as Minister of the Interior in April 1906 and quickly became its chairman – equivalent to prime minister – in July. Stolypin had the perfect background for the job of re-establishing political authority. During the revolutionary year of 1905 he had been governor of Saratov province, where he had displayed ruthless efficiency in dealing with revolutionary outbreaks. Now Stolypin had a major task on his hands. Although the 1905 revolution had been crushed, peasant unrest continued sporadically throughout 1906 and 1907.

In 1907, around 1200 government officials were murdered in terrorist attacks by revolutionaries. The attacks were launched by members of extremist groups such as the SRs. But Stolypin met terror with terror. Using field court martials, 1144 death sentences were handed out in the period between October 1906 and May 1907.

Stolypin also attacked the bases of revolutionary activity. Between 1906 and 1912 a thousand newspapers ceased publication and six hundred trade unions were forced to close. During 1908 and 1909 Stolypin's courts convicted 16,500 people of political crimes, of which 3600 were sentenced to death and 4500 to hard labour in prison camps. The impact of government action was impressive – in 1908 political assassinations by revolutionaries had fallen to 365. The restoration of law and order was one of Stolypin's great achievements. But he was not simply a reactionary – he also embarked on a series of very important reforms.

Take note

What evidence is there to suggest that Stolypin was a reformer?

Stolypin the reformer?

Stolypin, like other members of the government, was aware that social and economic reform was necessary in order to prevent another revolution (and preserve Tsarism). In particular he wanted to modernise Russian agriculture, not just to produce higher yields, but also to create a more prosperous class of peasant who he believed would be more loyal to the tsarist regime. From 1906 until his assassination in 1911, Stolypin embarked on a reform programme which transformed the Russian countryside. His key reform was the law of 9 November 1906, which freed peasants from the control of the commune. To leave a commune, a peasant no longer needed permission from the majority of its members. On 15 November the Peasant Land Bank was instructed to give loans to peasants who wanted to leave the commune, and as of New Year's Day, 1907, redemption payments were abolished. In June 1910 another reform dissolved all those communes where no redistribution of land had taken place since the Emancipation of the Serfs in 1861. Stolypin also encouraged peasants to move to the undeveloped agricultural areas of Siberia with the incentive of cheap land financed by government loans. Taken together, all these reforms laid the foundations for an independent Russian peasantry.

The impact of these reforms was considerable. In 1905 about 20 per cent of peasants had ownership over their own land, but by 1915 this figure had risen to 50 per cent. In addition, agricultural production rose from 45.9 million tonnes in 1906 to 61.7 million tonnes in 1913. Russian agriculture was clearly improving. However, these developments were severely disrupted by the First World War. Some historians have argued that had war not broken out, Russia could have developed a more stable. loyal and prosperous peasantry as Stolypin envisaged.

Although Stolypin brought great changes to the Russian countryside, little was done to improve the living and working conditions of Russia's industrial workers. Shortly after his assassination, Russia was plagued by another round of industrial unrest, beginning with the Lena Goldfield massacre of 1912 in Siberia, where strikers were killed by the police. From 1912 to 1914,

Peter Stolypin

(1862–1911)

Chairman of the Council of Ministers – the Prime Minister of Russia – from 1906 to 1911. He became known for his attempts to battle revolutionary groups and for introducing agrarian reforms. Stolypin hoped, through his reforms, to stem peasant unrest by creating a class of smallholding landowners. He is seen as one of the last major statesmen of Imperial Russia with a clearly defined political programme and determination to undertake major reforms. Stolypin cleverly manipulated the Duma to achieve a pro-government majority by the end of 1907. His land reforms and reforms in education helped modernise Russia. He was assassinated by a Socialist Revolutionary while visiting Kiev in 1911.

Russia was affected by strikes and demonstrations which had many of the characteristics of the early days of the 1905 Revolution. In June 1914 a general strike was called in Moscow. The wave of industrial unrest only came to an abrupt end with the outbreak of the First World War in August 1914.

Take note

As you read through this section, note down:

- The political makeup of each Duma, e.g. mainly liberal, or mainly conservative
- Government interference with the Duma or elections
- Key reforms passed by each Duma

The Dumas 1906–1914

According to the British historian, Orlando Figes, the period from 1906 to 1914 was a battle between parliamentary and royalists forces. After the 1905 Revolution supporters of the Tsar attempted to regain control. Others wanted to use the changes made during the Revolution to build a truly parliamentary system of government. The October Manifesto of 1905 offered support to both sides. Royalists saw it as a final change in the political system, while those on the left of Russian politics saw it as a beginning of more change. This conflict was played out in the State Duma.

The First Duma

Elections to the First Duma were done on a broad franchise, but both the Socialist Revolutionaries and Bolsheviks boycotted the elections. The largest groups elected were the Trudoviks – a loose collection of radicals who supported the workers and the peasants – followed by the Kadets and the Progressivists – a loose collection of liberal middle-class businessmen. All groups wanted to use the Duma to introduce further reforms, including land reform and the release of political prisoners. When these requests were refused, the Duma passed a vote of no confidence in the prime minister, Ivan Goremykin. The Duma was dissolved after only 72 days by the Tsar. It had made 391 requests against what it saw as illegal government action, but in the end only two resolutions were passed, one against capital punishment and the other in favour of famine relief. Given its hostility to the government, this Duma became known as the 'Duma of Public Anger'.

Tsar Nicholas II opens the first meeting of the Duma, St Petersburg, April 1906

How the Duma worked

Russia's first national parliament contained two houses:

- The Lower House was the State Duma. It could not enact laws unless it was supported by the Upper House and the Tsar.
- The Upper House was called the Council of State. Half of its membership were elected from zemstva, the Orthodox Church, the nobility and universities. The other half were chosen by the Tsar. The dominant group were the United Nobility, who acted as a block on Duma reforms. The Council of State was known as 'the graveyard of Duma hopes'.

The Vyborg Manifesto

Frustrated by this early dissolution, a group of Duma deputies went to Vyborg, in the province of Finland, near St Petersburg, and issued the 'Vyborg Manifesto' asking the Russian people to resist the Tsar's action through non-payment of taxes. But the plan backfired – the 200 deputies who made the manifesto were banned from standing for the next Duma.

The Second Duma

The Second Duma saw the number of Kadets halved, partly because so many of them were banned from standing for election after the Vyborg manifesto, although both the SRs and Social Democrats gained seats. Under the guidance of Stolypin, this Duma passed important land reform. But the Second Duma only lasted three months. The Duma sharply criticised the administration of the army which angered the Tsar and his supporters. Following this, the police framed radical members of the Duma for trying to encourage mutinies, providing the perfect excuse for the Tsar to dissolve the Duma.

Electoral reform and the Third and Fourth Dumas

To ensure that the government received greater support, the election to the next Duma was restricted to the wealthy – only the richest 30 per cent of the male population could vote. This excluded most of the reformers' supporters. As a result, the pro-government parties performed well, winning 287 out of the 443 seats. Stolypin used this third Duma to push through further land reform. Its pro-government views, however, meant that the radical opposition called it the 'Duma of Lords and Lackeys'.

In 1911 Stolypin was assassinated by a double agent working for the Okhrana, and Finance Minister Vladimir Kokovtsov took his place. The cautious Kokovtsov was very able and a supporter of the Tsar, but he could not compete with the powerful court factions that dominated the government, and the Fourth Duma of 1912–1914 was as conservative as its predecessor.

The first four Dumas

First Duma
April–June 1906 (The Duma of Public Anger)

Second Duma
February–June 1907

Third Duma
November 1907–June 1912 (The Duma of Lords and Lackeys)

Fourth Duma
November 1912–August 1914

Successes and failures

It is clear the Third and Fourth Dumas thwarted attempts at reform, such as the extension of the zemstva system into Poland or more religious toleration. However, because the Third and Fourth Dumas were not so radical, the government was more inclined to listen to them. The Third Duma served its full term and the Fourth Duma lasted right up until the outbreak of the First World War . During this time, the Dumas managed to bring in some successful reforms. For example:

- The Land Captains introduced in 1892 were replaced by justices of the peace.
- The government introduced a plan to have universal primary education within ten years.
- Health and accident insurance programmes were introduced for industrial workers.
- Improvements were made to the army and navy.

The Duma was never a truly parliamentary institution – and the government had never wanted it to be one. It was only a mixture of revolutionary pressure in 1905 and pressure from France (who provided Russia with large loans) that led to the creation of the Duma in the first place. Yet by 1914 political parties had been established legally and the Duma offered a major forum for political debate. Although the Dumas did not always succeed in influencing the Tsar or pushing through reforms, Duma debates were reported in the press. In this way, the reformers and radicals in the Duma had the opportunity to influence public opinion legitimately – something that had been denied to them previously as radical newspapers were often banned or subject to censorship.

Number of representatives in each of the Dumas

Political party	First Duma	Second Duma	Third Duma	Fourth Duma
Mensheviks	18	65	Nil	Nil
Bolsheviks	Nil	Nil	19	15
Social Revolutionaries	Nil	37	Nil	Nil
Trudoviks	136	104	13	10
Kadets	182	98	54	53
Octobrists	17	54	154	95
Progressivists	27	28	28	41
Rightists	8	10	147	154
National Minorities	60	93	26	22
Others	Nil	50	Nil	Nil

Taken from M. Lynch, *Reaction and Revolution*, Hodder Murray, 1992

Notes

- Mensheviks and Bolsheviks were two factions within the Social Democrat Party. The Bolsheviks boycotted the elections to the first Duma.
- Octobrists and Rightists were pro-government parties.
- Mensheviks, Bolsheviks, Socialist Revolutionaries and Trudoviks were radical groups.
- Trudoviks were a loose group of left-wing supporters of labour and the peasants.
- The Socialist Revolutionaries boycotted the elections to the first Duma. Many stood as Trudoviks.
- Progressivists were a party of businessmen.
- Rightists were supporters of the Tsar.
- National Minorities were supporters of the Poles, Finns and other national minorities.

Activity: The Dumas

1. In what ways do you think the ability of the Duma to make reforms was limited?
2. How far do you think Russia had moved in the direction of a parliamentary system of government by 1914?

Activity: Bringing stability to Russia

Work in small groups. Each group will need to defend the importance of one of the following in bringing stability to Russia after the 1905 Revolution:

- Political repression
- Land and education reform
- The Dumas

1. Each group picks a spokesperson to defend their case to the whole class.
2. Having heard the presentations, the class should then list these issues in order of importance in bringing stability, giving reasons for their choices.

Chapter 7 The First World War

Key questions

- Why did the Russian army suffer defeat by the end of 1916?
- How did the First World War affect politics in Russia?
- What impact did the First World War have on the Russian economy?

When war broke out in Europe, in August 1914, it brought an end to industrial unrest in Russia. The country united behind the Tsar and his government in an atmosphere of patriotism. At first, Russia performed well. In 1914 her armies invaded eastern Germany and eastern Austria–Hungary. But by the end of 1916 the Russian army was in retreat. The war also had a major effect on the position of the Tsar and his family. Under the influence of Rasputin, an unpopular adviser, the Tsarina became increasingly unpopular. Finally, Russia suffered serious economic dislocation because of the war. And by Christmas 1916 the country was entering a period of major crisis. At first it seemed that the war might strengthen tsarism, but by 1916 it was on the brink of collapse.

Russia's military performance, 1914–1916

The war began well for Russia. The country was filled with a strong sense of patriotism, with the majority of the population rallying behind the Tsar. Even students in St Petersburg, who had recently been protesting against the Tsar, found a new enemy and took to protesting outside the German embassy. However, these successes were short-lived. In August 1914, Russian armies entered East Prussia, the easternmost province of Germany. They also overran much of the Austro-Hungarian province of Galicia. The Russian advance forced the Germans to amend their war plan, the Schlieffen Plan. Army units destined for France were diverted to the Eastern Front, and at the end of August and the beginning of September the Russian advance was stopped at the Battle of Tannenburg, in which the German generals Hindenburg and Ludendorf won a crushing victory over the Russian generals Rennenkampf and Samsonov. By the time the battle ended, 30,000 Russian troops were killed or wounded – and 95,000 were captured. Only 10,000, mostly from the retreating flanks, managed to escape. The Germans suffered fewer than 20,000 casualties and captured over 500 guns. (Rather than report the loss of his army to the Tsar, Samsonov shot himself on 29 August 1914.) However, at the end of September the Russians surrounded the Austro-Hungarian fortress town of Przemysl. After a siege lasting more than four months, the Russians eventually captured the town and 110,000 prisoners. These military developments had a mixed effect on the popularity of the war at home.

1915 proved to be the turning point in the fighting on the Eastern Front.

Take note

Construct a timeline from the outbreak of war, in August 1914 to Christmas, 1916. On the timeline, identify Russian successes and Russian defeats.

Tsar Nicholas II blesses his troops, 1914.

> **Take note**
>
> How did entry into the First World War affect the Russian economy?

After their victory at the Battle of Tannenburg, the Germans defeated the Russians in the Battle of Lodz in December 1914. This was followed by the Austro-German forces' launch of the Gorlice–Tarnow Offensive in July 1915. By the end of 1915, Russian forces had been completely driven out of Russian Poland. These military reverses led Tsar Nicholas II to make one of his most disastrous decisions. In September 1915, after the loss of Poland, he dismissed his Uncle Nikolai as commander-in-chief of the Russian army and took command himself. Nicholas II was plainly unqualified to command a military unit, let alone a vast army of several millions. But from September 1915 Tsar Nicholas II took personal responsibility for Russia's military fortunes on the Eastern Front. In addition, while he was away at the Front, Nicholas II left the running of the government and the administration to his wife, the Tsarina Alexandra.

> **Take note**
>
> List the reasons why political opposition to the Tsar's government developed between August 1914 and December 1916.

From June to August 1916 the Russian forces launched their last major offensive of the war, the Brusilov Offensive. Initially, it met with success and even prompted Romania to enter the war on Russia's side. But by August the Brusilov Offensive had run out of momentum, and Russian forces had to retreat from the Baltic Sea to the Black Sea. This retreat was associated with desertions, and by Christmas 1916 the Russian army was facing major shortages of war material and a fall in morale.

A variety of reasons contributed to the failure of the Brusilov Offensive. Nicholas II proved to be a very poor commander-in-chief, and poor internal communications – the railways, in particular – led to a shortage of military equipment getting to the front. Historian Norman Stone has shown that the Russian economy was capable of performing well in war production. In September 1916, for example, the Russians produced 4.5 million artillery shells, compared to the German level of 7 million per month, and Germany was fighting a war on two fronts. But the problem for Russia was transportation, because it failed to get enough supplies to the battle areas. By the end of 1915, for instance, some Russian artillery units were limited to firing three shells per day because of these shortages.

By Christmas 1916, 1.6 million Russian soldiers were dead, 3.9 million were wounded and 2.4 million had been taken prisoner.

The Home Front

The war had an enormous impact on Russia. The country mobilised 5.3 million men – 9 per cent of the population – in 1914 and, by Christmas 1916, 15.3 million men had experienced military service. The cost of fighting the war and maintaining such a large armed force put great strains on the Russian state. The National Budget rose eightfold between 1913 and 1916, financed out of higher taxes, loans and borrowing from Britain and France. In order to pay for the war, the government printed more money, leading to inflation, with prices rising over 200 per cent between August 1914 and Christmas 1916.

The loss of agricultural workers and horses to the army put a great strain on the production of food. This, combined with the takeover of railway lines by the army, led to food shortages in towns and cities. Moscow, for example, had been receiving 2200 railway wagons of grain per month in 1914. But by Christmas 1916 this figure was down to around 300 wagons. As a result, the Russian Home Front faced a major economic crisis for the winter of 1916 1917. The huge loss of life and military humiliations also undermined domestic support for the war. As 1917 began, the Russian government was facing a massive crisis.

The political impact of the war in Russia

The rise in patriotism led to the creation of a number of important bodies to help with the war effort. At the beginning of the war, for example, the Union of Zemstva provided medical facilities for the army, and the Congress of Representatives of Industry and Trade helped co-ordinate war production. In July 1915 a Central War Industries Committee was created under the Octobrist, Guchkov. This was created by businessmen to help stimulate production of weapons and ammunition – something Russia badly needed.

These organisations were immensely successful and proved critical to the Russian war effort. However, to many people, the success of these organisations only served to highlight the incompetence of the government by comparison. Being an autocracy, the Tsar's government didn't know how to effectively incorporate these groups and political parties into its own war effort. In June 1915 the zemstva and town dumas formed ZEMGOR, the All-Russian Union of Zemstva and Cities to aid the care of war casualties. The government, however, failed to use the organisation officially, with the result

The Progressive Bloc

A group within the State Duma that wanted to see greater parliamentary control of the government. One of their major demands was the creation of ministerial responsibility to the Duma. This would have meant that government ministers were answerable for their actions to the Duma, rather than to the Tsar. This would have created a system of parliamentary government similar to Britain. Nicholas II constantly refused to meet this demand, mostly due to the adamant position of the Tsarina and Rasputin. Later, Guchkov claimed that members of the Progressive Bloc would consider a coup d'état, but they did not undertake any action. It soon became clear that nothing was able to save the monarchy, and Guchkov was among those who persuaded the Tsar to abdicate on 2 March 1917.

that ZEMGOR became a centre of liberal discontent against the shortcomings of the Russian war effort.

Fustrated at being unable to take a full and active part in the Russian war effort, 236 out of the 422 State Duma deputies formed themselves into the 'Progressive Bloc', comprising mainly Kadets, Octobrists and Progressivists. The Progressive Bloc called for a 'government of public confidence' in which ministers would be reponsible to the Duma. Although not a direct challenge to the Tsar and his authority, the Progressive Bloc became the centre of potential opposition.

A Russian cartoon shows Nicholas II and Alexandra as puppets of Rasputin

But rather than deal with this opposition effectively, Nicholas only made things worse. He would not listen to the demands of the Progressive Bloc and refused their requests for change. As a result most of the ministers who had campaigned for reform either resigned or were dismissed when Nicholas went to the Front in September 1915. With the Tsarina Alexandra in charge, there was even less hope of change. The Tsarina distrusted the Progressive Bloc and thought that organisations such as ZEMGOR and the War Industries Committee were disloyal. From then on, only ultra-conservative tsarists were appointed to ministerial positions. The result was that the Tsar and the government became even less popular.

The role of Rasputin

A further unsettling aspect of the Russian Home Front was the role of Gregory Rasputin, a Siberian Orthodox Monk and mystic who became involved with the Royal Court in 1907. The heir to the throne, the Tsarevich Alexei, had been diagnosed with haemophilia soon after his birth in 1904, and Rasputin was initially called in because he was believed to have the power of healing, (and there is evidence to suggest that Rasputin did, somehow, have the ability to offset the worst symptoms of haemophilia, such as internal bleeding.)

Gregory Rasputin

(1871–1916)

A Siberian 'starets' (holy man), Rasputin had been known to the Russian royal family since 1905, but his influence with them can be dated from 1907. His ability to 'cure' the Tsarevich gave him considerable influence with the religiously minded Tsarina, Alexandra. (The means by which he was able to do this have never been properly explained.) There were rumours about a sexual affair between Rasputin and the Tsarina – and about his extravagant lifestyle, including bouts of drunkenness which made him a public scandal. He was murdered by Russian noblemen in December 1916.

By 1914 Rasputin was a regular and significant member of the Court and, in particular, a personal confidant of the Tsarina, Alexandra. His main influence on Russia's performance in the First World War came after the Tsar went to the Front, as commander-in-chief, in September 1915. Alexandra was left to organise the government and administration.

Between September 1915 and December 1916 there were constant ministerial changes, many of which were seen as influenced by Rasputin. And as the Russian war effort faltered, more and more blame was laid at the foot of Alexandra who, as a German by birth, was accused of being in sympathy with the enemy.

By December 1916, if there was a movement for political change, it came from royalists who wanted to preserve the Tsarist regime through the removal of Rasputin. In December 1916, Rasputin was murdered by a group of nobles, who hoped that by his death they would aid the Russian war effort. But Russia's fortunes in the war continued to deteriorate, and now the only people to blame were the Tsar and Tsarina.

Activity: The crisis facing Russia

From the information contained in this chapter, give an explanation of how the following contributed to the crisis facing Russia at the end of 1916:

- Russia's military performance
- The impact of war on the economy
- The role of the Tsar and Tsarina
- Political opposition.

Chapter 8 **The February Revolution**

Key questions

- Why did demonstrations occur in Petrograd in February 1917?
- How did the demonstrations lead to a Revolution?
- Why did the Tsar abdicate?

In January 1917 there was little sign of revolution. Although the Tsar and Tsarina were deeply unpopular, none of the radical parties were plotting their immediate overthrow and the Progressive Bloc had ruled out staging a coup d'état. In fact, if the Tsar was under threat at all, it was mainly from those royalists who wanted to preserve the Tsarist autocracy and saw Nicholas II as too weak and indecisive. Yet by March 1917 three hundred years of Romanov rule in Russia had come to an end and the country had become a liberal republic under a Provisional Government. The events which led to this enormous change were not planned. The fall of Tsarism was due to a combination of factors, all associated with Russia's involvement in the First World War.

St Petersburg – Petrograd – Leningrad – St Petersburg

Petrograd was the new name given to St Petersburg after the outbreak of war in 1914. St Petersburg was the German spelling for the city, and a more patriotic Russian spelling was felt necessary. It was renamed Leningrad on Lenin's death in 1924, but when the Soviet Union collapsed in 1991, the city returned to its original name, St Petersburg.

Russian calendar

Before 1918, Russia used the Julian calendar, which was thirteen days behind the Gregorian calendar used by the rest of Europe. Therefore the 'February Revolution' occurred in early March, according to the rest of Europe. This book uses the Russian dates.

Take note

How did demonstrations and strikes develop in Petrograd by 24 February?

The Petrograd demonstrations

In the 1920s an American historian, W.H. Chamberlain, claimed that the February Revolution was 'one of the most leaderless, spontaneous, anonymous revolutions of all time'. It began as a series of uncoordinated demonstrations in the capital, Petrograd. On 9 January, 140,000 workers went on strike and demonstrated in the streets to commemorate the anniversary of Bloody Sunday, which had begun the 1905 Revolution. On the last day of January, strikes about food shortages occurred sporadically across Russia. On 14 February, 100,000 workers again went on strike in Petrograd, protesting against food shortages and poor working conditions. On the same day, the State Duma was reconvened and, instead of supporting the government, it attacked it over the food shortages. The government only made matters worse, however, by announcing on 19 February that bread rationing would start on 1 March. This news led to panic buying of various foodstuffs.

A key event was the demonstrations in Petrograd on 23 February to commemorate International Women's Day, when tens of thousand of women took to the streets. This coincided with a major strike at the Putilov

Engineering Works and, together, the demonstrators and the strikers numbered over 100,000.

The following day, 24 February, the strikes and demonstrations continued – mainly about food shortages and the threat of rationing. Soviets (committees) of workers were formed to formulate demands against the government. By 25 February the number of demonstrators had swelled to 200,000. It was at this stage that the government tried to take control of the capital's streets. The police arrested members of the Workers' Group, a leading body set up by workers in Petrograd to organise strikes and demonstrations. All newspapers were shut down and public transport ceased to operate.

Workers in Petrograd protesting against food shortages and demanding an 8-hour working day.

The defection of the armed forces

The turning point in the Revolution came on 25 February, when Cossack troops refused to fire on the demonstrators. The next day, troops did fire on the demonstrators, killing 40 of them, but the elite Pavlovsky Life Guards refused to carry out orders. This was the first significant sign that government authority had begun to break down. In the 1905 Revolution the Tsar's regime had survived because of the support of the armed forces. But now, at a critical time in the February Revolution, the army was beginning to desert the government. Disaffection spread further on the following day, when the Volinsky Regiment mutinied – and joined the demonstrators.

Take note

Describe how the events of 25 February to 2 March led to the fall of the Tsar.

In an attempt to reassert its authority, the government dissolved the State Duma. Instead of disbanding, however, the State Duma formed a twelve-man committee to take over the running of the country, and this became the Provisional Government. The Provisional Government was a self-proclaimed committee which eventually would form the first government of Russia following the fall of the Tsar.

What had begun as spontaneous demonstrations and strikes, mainly about food shortages, had become a political revolution. The Tsar began to lose his nerve, and on 28 February he telegrammed the State Duma, offering to share power. However, under the leadership of Mikhail Rodzianko, the State Duma refused the Tsar's offer.

On 1 March the workers' soviets which had begun forming on 24 February joined forces to make the Petrograd Soviet. This was a repeat of the events in the 1905 Revolution which saw the creation of the St Petersburg Soviet. It issued 'Order Number 1' which demanded that all officers in the army be elected by their men. This began the rapid deterioration of authority and command over the army.

The Tsar's decision to abdicate

On 1 March, the Tsar made a last bid to retake control. He boarded a train at his army HQ in Mogilev in an attempt to get back to Petrograd. However, on 2 March his train was stopped at Pskov, 250 km short of Petrograd, because anti-government soldiers had gained control of the railway line. In a siding at Pskov, Tsar Nicholas II was visited by members of the State Duma and was asked to abdicate. The Tsar agreed, and also abdicated the throne on behalf of the Tsarevich, his haemophiliac son Alexei, whom he feared would be too ill to serve as Tsar. Although Nicholas II was not technically allowed to abdicate for his son, he passed his throne to his own brother, Grand Duke Michael. On 3 March, however, Grand Duke Michael refused the offer of the throne – and by this act Russia ceased to be a monarchy. The Romanov dynasty, which had ruled Russia since 1613, had come to an abrupt end. On the same day, Prince Lvov was announced prime minister in charge of the Provisional Government.

In the space of just two weeks the unplanned demonstrations had resulted in political revolution.

Timeline for the February Revolution

1917	
9 January	Strike to commemorate Bloody Sunday in Petrograd; strikes in other cities.
31 January	Strikes across Russia.
14 February	100,000 workers strike in Petrograd. The State Duma is reconvened.
19 February	Petrograd authorities announce that bread will be rationed from 1 March.
23 February	Demonstrations in Petrograd for International Women's Day.
24 February	The strikes continue and grow ever larger. Small numbers of soviets begin forming.
25 February	Over 200,000 people are now on strike in Petrograd. Cossack troops fight police to protect protestors.
26 February	The Tsar orders the use of military force to break the strike. Troops of the Volynski Guard Regiment fire on protestors causing tens of casualties, but other troops of the Petrograd garrison begin to mutiny later in the day. The State Duma is suspended.
27 February	The Petrograd garrison mutinies, joins the protestors and begins arming themselves. The State Duma refuses to disband.
28 February	The Tsar tries to return to Petrograd but becomes stuck in Pskov.
1 March	The Petrograd Soviet issues 'Order Number 1'.
2 March	The Tsar abdicates on behalf of himself and his son (which was technically illegal) in order to help both the war and peace.
3 March	Michael Romanov, brother of the Tsar and now heir, rejects the throne.
March–April	The February Revolution spreads across Russia, with mini dumas (public committees) taking control of official, government and police matters, while workers and soldiers create parallel soviets. Committees form for just about everything.

Taking it further

To what extent was the February Revolution an example of the failure of the Tsar's government to deal effectively with strikes and demonstrations in Petrograd?

Activity: Comparing Revolutions

1. Compare the events of the 1905 Revolution (see Chapter 5) and the February 1917 Revolution. In what ways were they similar? In what ways were they different?

   You could use a venn diagram like this one to help you note down your ideas. Note similarities in the area that overlaps and differences in each side.

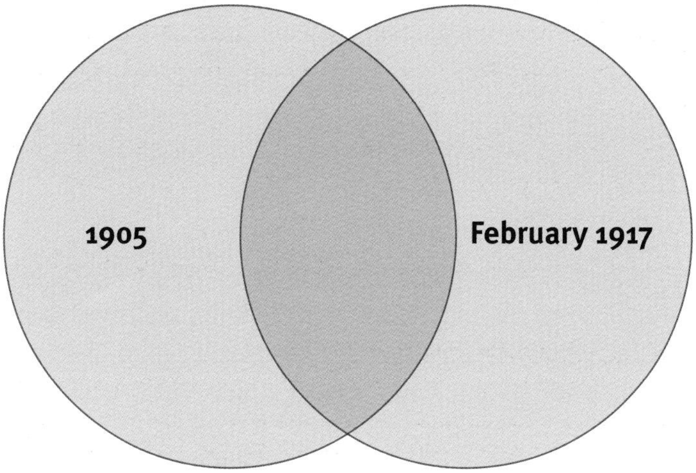

2. What do you regard as the main reasons why the Tsar fell from power in February 1917?

Skills Builder 2: Planning answers to questions on causation and change

Questions on causation

In the AS examination you may be asked questions on causation – questions about what caused historical events to take place.

Some may ask you to explain why something happened. For example:

> (A) Why did the strikes and demonstrations of February 1917 lead to a political revolution?

Other questions on causation will ask you to assess the importance of a reason for an event, in relation to other reasons. These often begin with 'How far...?' or 'To what extent...?'. Here is an example:

> (B) How far do you agree that the First World War was mainly responsible for the February Revolution of 1917?

Planning your answer

Before you write your essay you need to make a plan. In the exam you will have to do this very quickly! The first thing to do is to identify what information you may wish to put in your answer. Let's look at some examples.

When planning an answer to Question (A) you could first note down reasons other than the strikes and demonstrations which explain why February Revolution took place. You can do this in different ways. For example, you could:

- Write a list all the reasons you can remember why the February Revolution took place.
- Draw a 'mindmap' with 'February Revolution' at the centre, and surround it with all the reasons you can remember.
- Then draw arrows to link your reasons to show how factors combined with the strikes and demonstrations to lead to the Tsar's loss of control.

When planning an answer to Question (B) you need to think about the importance of each reason. You could:

- Write a list of all the reasons, then number them in order of importance.
- Draw a mindmap with 'February Revolution' at the centre and put the most important reasons near the middle and the least important reasons further away.

Remember, in the examination you are more likely to have questions which ask you to think about the most important reasons, but you will need to be able to explain why something happened in order to think about the relative importance of the causes that you list.

The information you require for these answers can be found in Chapter 7 and Chapter 8. Go to Chapter 7 and identify reasons where the First World War created the conditions which made a revolution likely to occur. Then go to Chapter 8 and identify other reasons which brought about the February Revolution.

Linking the causes

Once you have identified the relevant information and organised it, it is important to see links between the reasons.

In making your plan, try grouping reasons together which have links. If you have produced a list of reasons, you may want to rearrange the points where you can identify clear links between them. If you have drawn a 'mindmap', you could draw arrows between the linked points.

Writing your answer

For Question (A) above, you could write a paragraph on each cause which contributed to Nicholas' weak position in 1917, perhaps dealing with long-term causes and short-term causes separately. Remember, though, to show how they combined to bring about the end of Romanov dynasty.

For Question (B) above, you should build up an argument on the relative importance of different causes, focusing particularly on the role of the First World War. Remember to answer the question! You might want to deal with the First World War first and then assess the importance of other points in bringing about the February Revolution. Make sure you write a separate paragraph for each reason that you identify.

In your concluding paragraph, make sure that you reach a judgement on 'how far' the First World War was the main cause of the February Revolution.

Questions about change

These questions will require you to explain how far a historical event brought about change. Examples of this type of question would be:

(C) How extensive were the political and economic changes in Russia in the years 1906–1914?

(D) How far did the economic position of peasants improve between 1881 and 1914?

Planning your answer

When you plan, organise your material in a way that will help you to answer the question.

For instance, for Question (C) draw up two lists. One list should contain information on where politics and the economy changed between 1906 and 1914. The other list would contain information on where politics and the economy did not change.

Alternatively, you could produce two 'mindmaps'. One will have 'Areas of political and economic change' in the centre. The other would have 'Areas where political and economic affairs stayed the same' in the centre. Around each of these mindmaps identify the points which you feel are relevant.

Don't organise your material in a chronological way. This would encourage the writing of descriptive or narrative-style answers. Such answers may contain lots of accurate and relevant historical information, but your factual knowledge and evidence must be used *to support an argument.*

Writing your answer

In Questions (C) and (D) you are asked 'how extensive' and 'how far' in relation to changes. So in your final paragraph, the conclusion, you will be expected to *make a judgement*. Based on the historical evidence you have presented in your answer, you will be able to decide whether the weight of evidence is stronger on the 'change' side of the argument or on the other side.

Remember, you need to produce a answer which has a balanced structure, where you use historical knowledge as evidence 'for' or 'against' change.

Activity: How much have you learned?

Here are some examples of questions which deal with causation and change. First, identify the causation questions and give a reason to support your choice. Then identify the questions which deal with change and give a reason for your choice. Finally, choose one 'causation' question and one 'change' question and produce a plan for each, showing how you would organise your answer.

(E) To what extent did Alexander III reverse the reforms of his predecessor, Alexander II?

(F) How far did the Dumas improve the political system of Russia in the period 1906–1914?

(G) How far was Nicholas II responsible for his own downfall?

Chapter 9 The Provisional Government

Key questions

- What problems did the Provisional Government face in Russia?
- What impact did the war have on the Provisional Government?
- Why was the Provisional Government so short-lived?

In March 1917 Russia ceased to be an empire – the Tsar had abdicated and Russia became a republic. In place of the Tsar's government there was now a Provisional Government made up of members of the State Duma. As its name suggests, this was an interim government which was to rule Russia until such time that a new constitution could be drawn up. Yet the new Provisional Government was warmly welcomed by Russia's wartime allies, Britain and France, and the First World War now became a war between a German military dictatorship and a group of democratic countries. From the outset, however, the Provisional Government faced enormous problems. It had taken over the government of Russia in the middle of a world war and a major economic and political crisis. For almost eight months the Provisional Government grappled with these problems, but by October 1917 it had lost much of its authority within Russia and it faced the prospect of replacement by more radical elements in Russian politics.

Take note

Using a table like the one below, list the problems faced by the Provisional Government, the actions it took, and whether they succeeded or not. Put each problem in the appropriate section of the table. The first one has been filled in for you.

The problems faced by the Provisional Government in March 1917

Political authority

An immediate problem facing the Provisional Government was one of legitimacy. It comprised members of the State Duma who had formed a Provisional Committee to demand reform from the Tsar. Once the Tsar abdicated, the Provisional Government became the replacement government of Russia. It was dominated by members of the Octobrist and Kadet parties which, in terms of popular following, were a minority group. The only representative of a radical party was a lawyer called Alexander Kerensky. Neither the Menshevik or Bolshevik factions of the Social Democrats or the Socialist Revolutionaries were included.

Problems facing the Provisional Government

Problem	*What action did the Provisional Government take?*	*Success or failure?*
Government 1. There were two governments – The Provisional Government and the Soviet.	The Provisional Government did nothing to try to end the power of the Soviets.	Failure – because this undermined the authority of the Provisional Government.
Social and economic conditions		
Peasants		
First World War		

The Provisional Government also faced a rival for political power. During the February Revolution, soviets of workers, soldiers and sailors had developed spontaneously and then quickly formed themselves into a united Petrograd Soviet. By June 1917 the Petrograd Soviet developed into an All-Russia Soviet. Like the Provisional Government, the All-Russia Soviet claimed the right to issue laws for Russia. One of its early decisions had a profound effect on the army. 'Order Number 1' of the Petrograd Soviet had required all officers in the army to be elected by their own troops. This had the effect of undermining the authority of officers. Unpopular and/or enthusiastic officers were dismissed. By the time of the June Offensive the Russian Army on the Eastern Front was not in a position to launch a successful offensive against the German and Austro-Hungarian armies.

From February to October 1917 the Provisional Government shared political power with the Soviet, with major areas of policy having to be agreed by both. There were some links between the two. In May 1917, for example, six members of the Soviet were included in the Provisional Government, including Skobelev (Minister of Labour). However, the politician with the best links between the two bodies was Alexander Kerensky, and from July 1917 Kerensky became prime minister and head of the Provisional Government. Yet both bodies viewed each other with suspicion. The Provisional Government remained throughout its existence as a mainly liberal body. The Soviet, in contrast, was dominated by left-wing groups, such as Socialist Revolutionaries and Social Democrats. This contrast became more pronounced as time went on with the more radical groups gaining an ever greater share of influence in the Soviet. By October 1917 the dominant Social Democrat group in the Soviet was the Bolsheviks, overtaking the more moderate Mensheviks. Order Number 1 also stated that the military orders of the Provisional Government would only be recognised if they were agreed by the Soviet. This tipped the balance of power away from the Provisional Government as the Soviet had effective control over the army.

The Petrograd Soviet in session at the Tauride Palace, 1917.

Early reforms of the Provisional Government

When the Provisional Government took power it was welcomed by the western Allies, Britain and France. To them the revolution meant Russia would become a liberal, democratic regime. The war would become a conflict between democracy on one side and military dictatorship, in the form of Germany, on the other. As a result, the Provisional Government began implementing reforms which it hoped would lay the foundations for a new liberal, democratic Russia. Crucially, the Soviet agreed with these early reforms. These included:

- Freedom of the press
- Abolition of the Okhrana, the secret police
- Release of all political prisoners
- Religious freedom
- Preparations for the calling of a Constituent Assembly to draw up a new democratic constitution for Russia.

The war

The biggest problem facing the Provisional Government effectively was the First World War. By March 1917 Russia had already lost territory in Poland and western Russia. Millions of Russian soldiers had been killed, wounded or taken prisoner. Morale within the armed forces was low, and the mutinies by both soldiers and sailors had contributed to the collapse of the Tsarist government in the February Revolution.

However, the Revolution was welcomed by Russia's wartime allies, Britain and France, who now hoped that the Russian commitment to fighting Germany would improve. Like many Russians, the western Allies believed that the Tsar had been a major obstacle to the effective prosecution of the war by Russia. Within weeks of the February Revolution, the Provisional Government was visited by British and French politicians and bankers, aiming to ensure Russia's continued participation in the war. Russia owed large amounts of money in foreign loans, and the British and French banks were willing to continue loaning money as long as Russia continued fighting.

There were many within the Provisional Government who believed that Russia had a duty to stay in the war. The foreign minister, Paul Milyukov, supported the idea that Russia's future lay with victory over Germany – on the side of western democracies like Britain and France. For a time, morale in the armed forces improved. The soldiers and sailors were now fighting for democracy rather than the Tsarist autocracy. But the improvement in morale did not last long because the army still suffered supply problems and the economy continued to deteriorate.

The continuation of the war brought the Provisional Government into conflict with the Soviet, which had issued an 'Address to the People of the Whole World, declaring for peace without annexations and indemnities' on 14 March 1917. This meant that they would support the continuation of the war but only to stop Germany taking over and crushing the revolution. They would not support continuing the war for any other reason, such as to gain land or money from their defeated opponents (indemnities). This ran counter to the war aims of the Provisional Government, who hoped to gain territory at the expense of the Ottoman Empire. Relations between the Soviet and the Provisional Government worsened when the Provisional

Government reassured the Allies that it would continue fighting on the same terms as before. In April 1917 demonstrations against the war began in Petrograd, leading to the resignation of Milyukov and the war minister, Guchkov, early in May.

The Provisional Government, in order to win support at home and abroad, planned an offensive on the Eastern Front. The 'June Offensive' was to be made against the Austro-Hungarian army on the south-western front in Galicia, where Russia had won major victories in 1914. The offensive began on 16 June in an attack on Lvov, in western Ukraine, and for two days the Russian troops advanced. But then the offensive started to break down. On 18 June the German and Austro-Hungarian counter-attacks led to mass desertions by the Russian troops. (Brusilov, their commanding general, had already warned the Provisional Government about the questionable morale of many of his regiments.) In one night, the elite units of the Eleventh Army captured 12,000 deserters, and reports came in of troops firing on their own officers and engaging in looting. From this point on, mid-June 1917, the Russian army began to collapse.

This was to be a fatal blow to the authority of the Provisional Government. It led directly to the 'July Days', a series of riots and demonstrations in Petrograd, similar to the February Revolution. Although the demonstrations were put down, the Provisional Government under Prince Lvov did not survive.

A new Provisional Government was formed, with a more radical composition. Kerensky, the SR lawyer, became the new (and last) prime minister of the Provisional Government. And now there was an increase in representation from the All-Russia Soviet in the Provisional Government.

Crisis in the countryside

The collapse of the Tsarist autocracy led to a collapse of administration across Russia. The Provisional Government had control of Petrograd and other major cities, but little control over the countryside. As a result, the peasants began to take the law into their own hands. Some peasants took over land from large landowners, while others engaged in violence against landowners. In June 1917 alone, the Provisional Government received over 700 complaints about illegal attacks on property. Following the collapse of the June Offensive, peasant soldiers returned from the Front to assist in this process of land redistribution. Without any direction from above, a social and economic revolution was taking place in the Russian countryside. By the end of summer 1917, Russia was entering a period of chaos. Peasants took land from the landowners and distributed it amongst themselves. The Provisional Government simply lacked the ability to impose its authority outside towns and cities. The army was in the process of disintegration. Most of the Russian countryside did not have an effective government at all.

Activity: Impact of the early reforms

Taking it further

'The Provisional Government lasted such a short time because it failed to deal with the social and economic problems it faced.' How far do you agree with this statement?

In what ways do you think the early reforms of the Provisional Government helped change Russia into a liberal, democratic regime?

Chapter 10 **The return of Lenin**

Key questions

- What were Lenin's political ideas?
- What were the April Theses?
- What impact did Lenin's return have on the Russian Revolution?

When the February Revolution took place, Lenin was in exile in Switzerland. In fact, he first read about the revolution in a Swiss newspaper. It came as a complete surprise to Lenin and his fellow Bolshevik exiles, and he was determined to return to Russia by any means. In the end, he accepted transportation from the German government to return to Russia, via Germany and Sweden.

Lenin's return, in April 1917, was to transform the political situation in Russia.

According to the British historian, Beryl Williams, 'Lenin's interpretation of Marxism came to dominate much of the world. His impact not just on Russia but on world history in the 20th century is incalculable.' Her view is supported by American historian, Richard Pipes, who stated, 'His strength of will, indomitable discipline, energy, and unshakeable faith in the cause had an effect that can only be conveyed by the overused word "charisma".' Of all the politicians in Russian history from 1881 to 1924, Lenin had the clearest vision of want he wanted to achieve. His ambition was nothing short of a complete political, social and economic revolution in Russia, as a prelude to worldwide revolution. Without Lenin there would have been no October Revolution of 1917 and no Communist Russia.

Lenin's political ideas

By 1917 Lenin was a committed follower of Karl Marx (see Chapter 4). Marxist ideas suggested that history would follow a pre-determined path, leading eventually to a communist society. On this path, society would go through clearly defined stages. By the nineteenth century most of western Europe had entered what Marx called the bourgeois, capitalist stage of development, where society was divided into the industrial workers (the proletariat), and the owners of production and commerce (the bourgeoisie). This phase would be replaced by the creation of a socialist society based on equality.

Like many university-educated Russians at the end of the nineteenth century, Lenin was attracted by these ideas. But the Russia of 1900 was far removed from the bourgeois, capitalist phase. About 80 per cent of Russians were peasants engaged in agriculture, and industry – where it existed – was limited in development. How then could Russia become a socialist society in Lenin's lifetime?

Lenin found a solution. He suggested that, instead of the industrial working

Take note

How did Lenin's return change the course of the Russian Revolution?

class leading a socialist revolution, this role would be taken by a small, disciplined party of professional revolutionaries, a 'vanguard' party at the head of the revolution. Lenin's views were so strong on this issue that he caused a split in the Russian Social Democrat Party in 1903. Lenin's faction – the Bolsheviks – were to be the vanguard party.

Lenin, however, faced many problems. Much of the Bolshevik leadership, including him, lived outside Russia. And within Russia the Bolsheviks were an illegal organisation, hounded by the Okhrana, the secret police.

The 1905 Revolution came as a complete surprise to Lenin, and the Bolsheviks played only a marginal role in it. In 1914, Lenin welcomed the outbreak of the First World War, hoping that the social and economic demands of the war would cause socialist revolution across Europe. Yet, in February 1917, Lenin was as surprised as other Russian exiles to read about the sudden outbreak of revolution and the fall of the Tsar.

Lenin's major writings, 1902–1917

What is to be Done? (1902)

This pamphlet advocated the creation of a disciplined party of professional revolutionaries to lead the socialist revolution in Russia. He took the title from Populist writer N.G. Chernyshevsky who wrote a novel in which the leading character, Rakhmetov, was a professional revolutionary.

Imperialism, the Highest Stage of Capitalism (1916)

This pamphlet was Lenin's contribution to the Marxist explanation of the outbreak of the First World War. Lenin believed capitalism led to the creation of large monopolies or cartels which dominated various parts of industry. These groups, in order to gain more economic power, would force their government to resort to war. To Lenin, this marked the beginning of the end of capitalism. Lenin also believed that socialist revolution would break out in the weakest, not strongest, capitalist economies. He had Russia in mind as 'capitalism's weakest link'.

Lenin's return to Russia

In February 1917 Lenin was living in exile in Zurich. Like other exiled Russian revolutionaries, Lenin was keen to get back to Russia. However, to do so he would have to cross enemy territory during a time of war. In March 1917 Lenin received permission from the German government to travel across Germany to neutral Sweden. Lenin and other revolutionaries were placed in a 'sealed train' – a train that was forbidden to stop or take on any other passengers. The train did stop to refuel, allowing Lenin the opportunity to talk with German socialist leaders, such as Karl Kautsky. From Sweden Lenin travelled to Finland, which was then part of the Russian Empire, and late on the night of 3 April, Lenin's train arrived in Petrograd. His arrival had been publicised in advance, and a large crowd awaited with expectation for his return. After leaving the train, Lenin addressed the crowd from the top of an armoured car parked outside the Finland Station. What he said came as a bombshell to all who heard him.

Just two months earlier, the Bolsheviks and their Social Democrat colleagues, the Mensheviks, had greeted the February Revolution with enthusiasm. As

Marxists they saw it as an important stage on the road to socialism, and they supported the creation of the Provisional Government and the Petrograd Soviet. This was seen as the bourgeois-capitalist stage of development which was an important prelude to eventual socialist revolution as set out in Marx's theories.

But Lenin now delivered a 90-minute speech where he roundly condemned the Provisional Government and demanded an immediate social revolution. His ideas were later published by the Bolshevik newspaper, *Pravda* (*Truth*) as the 'April Theses'.

The April Theses

In his speech on 3 April 1917 and in the April Theses, Lenin rewrote Marx's ideas. Lenin saw Russia as capitalism's weakest link. He also believed that a bourgeois revolution (which many recognised in the February Revolution) could be followed immediately by a socialist revolution. This ran counter to the views of the Bolshevik leadership in Petrograd. Kamenev and Stalin, for example, had both supported the Provisional Government.

So Lenin's first task was to win over the Bolsheviks in Russia to his view. He realised that the war was very unpopular and exploited this fact to gain support. He also saw that there was no opportunity for the Bolsheviks to participate in the Provisional Government, which was dominated by the Liberal parties. Instead, he suggested that political power should be handed over to the Soviets, where the Bolsheviks had support. Lenin's two main rallying cries 'Peace, Land and Bread' and 'All Power to the Soviets' were designed to both gain support for the Bolsheviks among the Russian population and undermine the Provisional Government. 'Peace, Land and Bread' was a popular message in a country exhausted by war and faced with serious food shortages. As well as highlighting the Provisional Government's support for the unpopular war, it also

A painting of Lenin's return to the Finland Station, Petrograd on the night of 3 April 1917.

The April Theses, published in *Pravda*, 7 April 1917

- The war is a greedy war for territory and should be ended immediately.
- The revolution is to move to its second stage, which must place power in the hands of the proletariat and the poor peasants.
- No support for the Provisional Government.
- The masses must be made to see that the Soviet is the only possible form of revolutionary government.
- Abolition of the police, the army and the bureaucracy. The salaries of all officials should not exceed the average wage of a worker.
- Confiscation of all landed estates from landowners and the aristocracy.
- Mass propaganda to win over the poor peasants and workers.
- The immediate union of all banks into a single national bank.
- All production of goods to come under Soviet control.
- An international organisation to be set up to spread revolution worldwide.

illustrated their failure to adequately address the land and food problems. Lenin's proposed solution, 'All Power to the Soviets' , played on the feeling amongst workers and peasants that the Provisional Government was made up entirely of landowners and the middle classes who would not look out for their interests.

To emphasise Bolshevik international credentials he suggested that a new international organisation should be formed. He also suggested an immediate and revolutionary transformation of Russian society. This would lead to worldwide socialist revolution.

The impact of Lenin's return

When he returned to Russia Lenin first had to win over his own party to his views. As the party's creator and main political thinker, Lenin had enormous influence. On 21 April, Lenin made his first bid for power, attempting to topple the Provisional Government through mass demonstrations. The Bolshevik Central Committee issued an order to send agitators to factories in Petrograd to whip up support, but only a small number of demonstrators went on the streets, and these were easily dispersed by the police.

On 9 June, the Bolsheviks tried again. This time they tried to exploit the unpopularity of the renewed fighting in the June Offensive on the eastern Front. But they failed to win support from the Petrograd Soviet for their views.

Although Lenin's early attempts to seize power failed, he continued to be a thorn in the side of the Provisional Government. For the rest of 1917 Lenin looked repeatedly for opportunities to increase Bolshevik support and oust the Provisional Government.

Activity: Lenin's return – I was there

Imagine you are a British reporter at the Finland Station on the night of 3 April 1917. Write an article on Lenin's speech from the armoured car. In your article refer to the ideas put forward by Lenin, how his speech was received by those who heard it at the Finland Station, and the likely effect that the speech would have on the Russian Revolution.

Taking it further

Find out more about how Lenin developed his political ideas by reading Section 1 'Did he help or hinder Russian socialism?' in *Lenin* by Derrick Murphy, Collins Flagship Historymakers, 2005.

Chapter 11 The July Days and the Kornilov Affair

Key questions

- Why did the July Days occur?
- What took place during the July Days?
- What impact did the July Days have for the Provisional Government and the Bolsheviks?

Since his return to Russia in April 1917, Lenin had been attempting to overthrow the Provisional Government. Following the failure of the June Offensive the popularity of the Provisional Government decreased. In early July demonstrations occurred in Petrograd, reminiscent of the previous February, and it seemed during these 'July Days' that the Government might fall. But the Provisional Government reasserted its authority when the army and the police dispersed the demonstrators.

The July Days resulted in a change in the Provisional Government. Prince Lvov resigned as prime minister, to be replaced by the more radical Alexander Kerensky. Also more radicals were admitted to the cabinet. The July Days also, temporarily, greatly damaged the Bolsheviks. They were accused of being major supporters of the demonstrations. Several Bolsheviks were arrested and Lenin fled to Finland, fearing that he would never again have the opportunity of overthrowing the Provisional Government.

Why did the July Days occur?

According to the American historian, Richard Pipes, 'no event in the Russian Revolution has been so wilfully lied about, the reason being that it was Lenin's worst blunder, a misjudgment that nearly caused the destruction of the Bolshevik Party'. To Richard Pipes the main culprit was Lenin, who planned the entire affair. A month earlier, in the All-Russia Congress of Soviets, Lenin had announced, to the surprise – and laughter – of many of the delegates, that the Bolsheviks were ready to take political power. Lenin, however, was undeterred. In June, the Provisional Government had launched a renewed attack on the Austro-Hungarian army. This was termed 'The June Offensive'. It was a complete disaster and led to mass desertions and a serious breakdown of discipline in the Russian Army. Believing the authority of the Provisional Government was critically weakened, Lenin used the failure of the June Offensive to plan a bid for power.

Take note

Construct a timeline of the July Days, highlighting what you think were the most important events.

What happened in the July Days of 3 to 6 July 1917?

On Monday 2 July, in the People's House in central Petrograd, a regimental concert was staged for the soldiers leaving for the Front, but it turned into an anti-government rally. There were demands that all political power should be handed to the Soviet. And that night the troops who had returned to their barracks formed a Provisional Revolutionary Committee to campaign against the government.

On Tuesday 3 July, machine-gunners from the First Machine Gun Regiment were sent to all the major Petrograd factories and military units to appeal for an uprising. By mid-afternoon thousands of workers and soldiers had taken to the streets. Demonstrations outside the Mariinsky Palace, the headquarters of the Provisional Government, and the Tauride Palace, the headquarters of the Petrograd Soviet, included slogans for the transfer of power to the Soviets. A large part of the demonstration went out of its way to parade past the Bolshevik headquarters at the Kshesinskaia mansion. According to British historian, Orlando Figes 'the crowd lacked leadership and direction. It did not quite know where it should go, or why. It had nothing but a "mood" – which wasn't enough to make a revolution'. Random rifle and machine-gun fire occurred throughout the city. Workers and soldiers appealed to the guards at the Peter and Paul Fortress, and with the guards' consent they were able to take it over. A group of soldiers made an unsuccessful attempt to capture war minister Alexander Kerensky.

Lenin in disguise after the failure of the July Days, August 1917.

However, the 3 July demonstrations brought the Provisional Government and the Soviet together. The Bolsheviks did not have a majority in the Soviet and many of the other parties in the Soviet did not trust them. Both the Provisional Government and the Soviet appealed for workers not to demonstrate on the streets, and they both saw the Bolsheviks as a threat to their authority. But several groups of soldiers chose to side with the demonstrators. Throughout the evening of 3 July the Provisional Government Cabinet and the Soviet Executive Committee met in a bid to restore order.

On Wednesday 4 July, the Bolsheviks supported more demonstrations. The Bolsheviks had infiltrated many of the factory committees set up in Petrograd after the February Revolution, and they now used their position to get the workers in these factories to demonstrate. The demonstrations continued throughout the day, with occasional clashes with the police. At the height of the demonstration, 50,000 armed people surrounded the Tauride Palace, waiting for an order to occupy it. But no order came, and in the evening, during a thunderstorm, the crowd dispersed. This was the turning-point of the 'uprising'.

In the early morning of Thursday 5 July, the Cabinet of the Provisional Government sent loyal troops from the Front back into Petrograd to restore order. These troops won over other soldiers who had stayed neutral during the demonstrations. In the late afternoon the Central Committee of the Bolshevik Party called off the demonstrations.

On the morning of Saturday 6 July, a large force of loyal troops, equipped with eight armoured cars and heavy artillery, surrounded the Bolshevik headquarters at the Kshesinskaia mansion. The 500 Bolsheviks inside

Take note

Describe how the failure of the July Days affected Lenin and the Bolsheviks.

surrendered – and were arrested. A warrant went out for Lenin's arrest but he had already fled Petrograd for the Finnish border, disguising himself by shaving off his beard, wearing a wig, and carrying a false ID card.

Glossary:

Coup d'état

Literally means overthrow of the State. A seizure of political power.

How did the July Days affect the Bolsheviks?

The July Days proved to be a major setback for the Bolsheviks. It was Lenin's idea to try to overthrow the Provisional Government through demonstrations, in the way that the Tsar's government had been overthrown by demonstrations during the February Revolution. Instead, he helped unite the Provisional Government and the Soviet against the Bolsheviks. Lenin was now accused of being a German spy and in the pay of the German government. The fact that he had required German permission to return to Russia in April 1917 added fuel to this view. Lenin was accused of high treason and branded a traitor. Once it was clear that the July demonstrations had failed, Lenin fled Petrograd. The Bolshevik organisation in Petrograd was in tatters – all its leaders were either in prison or on the run. Whilst he was in hiding in Finland, Lenin wrote *The State and Revolution*, a book in which he almost concedes the idea that a revolution in the near future was out of the question.

Take note

Show how the Kornilov Affair undermined the authority of the Provisional Government.

The aftermath of the July Days

The Kornilov Affair, August 1917

By August 1917 Russia seemed on the verge of chaos. Peasants were seizing land, industrial production was falling, soldiers were deserting, and the German and Austro-Hungarian armies were advancing. In that month the Germans captured Riga on the Baltic coast, which was regarded as a major military defeat. However, the Provisional Government had survived the demonstrations of the July Days and the Bolsheviks were temporarily out of the way.

What brought about a fatal blow to the position of the Provisional Government was the 'Kornilov Affair'. On 18 July, Brusilov was dismissed as commander in chief of the army after the failed June Offensive. He was replaced by General Lavr Kornilov. One of the enduring myths of 1917 was the belief that Kornilov planned a coup d'état against the Provisional Government in a bid to replace it with a more authoritarian regime. But the truth was that Kornilov was loyal and was more concerned about a possible left-wing radical plot against the Government, along the lines of another 'July Days'. To forestall such a development, Kornilov ordered Russian troops into Petrograd on 24 August 1917. But instead of seeing this as an act of support from his army, prime minister Kerensky panicked, fearing a military takeover. He ordered the arrest of Kornilov and he armed groups of workers in the capital, many of them Bolsheviks. Many Bolsheviks were also released from prison for the same purpose. And Kornilov never made it to Petrograd. By 1 September the whole affair was over, but it had a devastating effect on the Provisional Government who looked very weak in the light of the events. Support for them fell, while support for the All-Russia Soviet increased,

Lavr Kornilov

(1870–1918)

A Russian general who was of Cossack origin and had served with distinction in the Russo-Japanese War of 1904–1905. He was appointed head of the Petrograd Garrison by the Provisional Government after the February Revolution. In July 1917 he became commander in chief of the Russian army. His attempt to restore order in Petrograd, in August 1917 was misinterpreted as an attempted seizure of power. After the Bolshevik seizure of power in October 1917 he became a general in the White Army, and was killed in action in the Civil War.

with the main beneficiaries of the Kornilov Affair being the Bolsheviks. The fact that Kerensky had relied on them made the Bolsheviks look strong and set them up as the defenders of Petrograd and their numbers increased dramatically.

By October 1917 the Provisional Government had lost most of its authority. Contemporaries believed it would be replaced sooner rather than later – but no one knew exactly who would replace it.

Activity: Producing propaganda posters

Taking it further

Using information contained in this chapter, answer the following question:
Do the two historians, Richard Pipes and Orlando Figes, have similar views on the July Days? Give reasons to support your answer.

Produce two propaganda posters, one in support of the July Days and the Bolsheviks, the other against the July Days. You might consider using one of these ideas:

- Support the new Provisional Government
- End the war
- Incompetence of the Government
- All power to the Soviets
- Lenin, a German spy
- Defend Mother Russia against enemies

Chapter 12 The Bolshevik seizure of power

Key questions

- Who organised the Bolshevik seizure of power?
- How was it organised?
- Was it a mass uprising or the work of a small group of revolutionaries?

On the evening of 25 October 1917 the Bolsheviks occupied important parts of Petrograd as part of a planned takeover of power. The main part of the takeover was the capture and arrest of the Provisional Government, as it met in the Winter Palace. The signal for the attack was the firing of blank shells from the Cruiser *Aurora*, docked in the River Neva opposite the Palace. In the 1927 Soviet film, *October*, the director Sergei Eisenstein shows thousands of Bolsheviks storming the Winter Palace. But the reality was very different. The Winter Palace was defended by some junior officer cadets and a women's battalion – and the takeover was virtually bloodless. On the following morning Russians woke up to find they had a new government. Little did they know that the new government would introduce the most radical transformation ever seen in Russian society.

The rise in Bolshevik support

Take note

How did the Bolsheviks plan for a takeover of political power?

After the July Days, Bolshevik support dropped dramatically as the Provisional Government regained control. However, by October 1917, the situation had been transformed. In August, the Kornilov Affair led to fears of a right-wing military takeover and, as a result, the Bolsheviks were no longer seen as a threat but as defenders of the Revolution. The Affair also completely undermined the authority of the prime minister, Kerensky.

Following the July Days, Lenin supported a new programme of 'Peace, Bread, Land'. Peace referred to the Bolshevik opposition to the war; bread referred to the need to end food shortages in the towns and cities, and land referred to Bolshevik support for land seizures by the peasantry. These slogans drew support to Bolsheviks from both industrial workers and poor peasants, and by the time of the Kornilov Affair, Bolshevik membership had risen to 200,000, with the party producing 41 different newspapers across Russia. The party had also recruited an elite force of 10,000 'Red Guards' in Petrograd's factories. This group had been able to acquire arms during the Kornilov Affair, when Kerensky was preparing to defend the capital against the general.

The timing of the seizure of power

On 9 August an important announcement was made by the Provisional Government. It proposed a timetable for national elections to a Constituent Assembly. This assembly would have the task of producing a new constitution. The elections would take place on 12 November and the opening session of the Constituent Assembly would be on 28 November. Lenin was well aware that the Social Revolutionaries were likely to win the most votes and seats in the elections. If the Bolsheviks wished to seize power, therefore, they had to do so before the elections.

Following his return to Petrograd, Lenin developed his tactics. He suggested that all political power should be handed over to the All-Russia Soviet, where the Bolsheviks had a large amount of support. By the end of September, for the first time, the Bolsheviks had a majority of seats in the Petrograd Soviet. As the Provisional Government became more and more unpopular, the All-Russia Soviet became the one national institution which maintained the respect of the population. On 10 October Lenin left his hiding place to enter Petrograd to meet the Central Committee of the Bolshevik Party. After a heated debate, Lenin was able to persuade the Committee that an armed takeover of power should take place, although two leading Bolsheviks, Lev Kamenev and Gregory Zinoviev, opposed this move. The planning of the takeover was put in the hands of Leon Trotsky, a leading Social Democrat who had joined the Bolsheviks in May. Lenin hoped to hide Bolshevik involvement by handing over the planning to the Military Revolutionary Committee of the Petrograd Soviet.

Take note

Construct a timeline of the Bolshevik seizure of power, identifying what you think were the most important events.

Leon Trotsky

(1879–1940)

Born Lev Bronstein. Became involved in revolutionary activity as a teenager, was arrested and exiled to Siberia, but he escaped in 1902 to join the Social Democrats. He was initially an opponent of Lenin, but joined with the Bolsheviks in May 1917 after the April Theses. He became chair person of the Military Revolutionary Committee of the Petrograd Soviet. It was his plan that was so successfully executed by members of the Red Guards on 25 and 26 October, which led to an almost bloodless takeover of power.

The seizure of power

The events which led to the seizure of power were started by the Provisional Government. On the morning of 24 October it attempted to close down two Bolshevik newspapers in Petrograd. That evening, Lenin arrived at Bolshevik Party headquarters to put his plan to seize power into action immediately, because he feared that the Provisional Government was trying to clamp down on Bolshevik activity. Using the Military Revolutionary Committee (MRC) of the Petrograd Soviet, the Bolsheviks planned to takeover the capital on the eve of the Second Congress of the All-Russia Soviet on 26 October. The MRC was under the control of Leon Trotsky, and when they seized power they would announce that they had done so on behalf of the Soviet.

On the evening of 24 October MRC units and Red Guards occupied key areas of Petrograd and arrested most of the Provisional Government, who were in the Winter Palace. The only opposition they faced was a company of women soldiers and some officer cadets, who put up only minimal resistance. The members of the Provisional Government who were arrested did not offer any resistance. And all these activities went by unnoticed by the vast majority of the population of Petrograd.

At 10.00 a.m. the following day, 25 October, the MRC announced:

The Provisional Government has been deposed. State power has passed into the hands of the organ of the Petrograd Soviet of Workers' and Soldiers' Deputies – the Revolutionary Military Committee, which heads the Petrograd proletariat and the garrison.

The cause for which the people have fought, namely, the immediate offer of a democratic peace, the abolition of landed proprietorship, workers' control over production, and the establishment of Soviet power – this cause has been secured.

Long live the revolution of workers, soldiers and peasants!

The Military Revolutionary Committee of the Petrograd Soviet

This body was established on 16 October to protect the Soviet against a possible German advance on the city. By October 1917 it was chaired by Trotsky, with other Bolsheviks comprising 48 out of its 66 membership.

During that morning, Kerensky escaped from Petrograd in a car, put at his disposal by the US Embassy, in a bid to raise loyal troops to crush the Bolshevik takeover. That afternoon, the Russian Parliament was dispersed by Red Guards.

On the evening of 25 October, delegates to the All-Russia Soviet began meeting at the Smolny Institute. The next day, Lenin was able to announce to the All-Russia Soviet that the Provisional Government had been overthrown. The 390 Bolshevik representatives in the All-Russia Soviet were only too keen to accept Lenin's actions. The Mensheviks had only 80 seats and the Socialist Revolutionaries had 180. The All-Russia Soviet therefore endorsed the Bolshevik takeover.

Lev Kamenev

(1883–1936)

A leading Bolshevik who was in exile with Lenin from 1907 to 1914. He opposed the October Revolution to the point where he publicised his opposition in the press, which alerted the Provisional Government to the possibility of a coup d'état.

Bolsheviks troops occupy the Winter Palace.

Gregory Zinoviev

(1883–1936)

He joined the Bolsheviks in 1903 and was in exile with Lenin until 1917. He openly opposed the October Revolution and later resigned from Lenin's first government because Lenin wanted a coalition with Left Socialist Revolutionaries.

The reasons for Bolshevik success

Changing circumstances

In the spring of 1917 the Bolsheviks seemed to be the most unlikely group to overthrow the Provisional Government. Before Lenin's return, the leading Bolsheviks in Russia – such as Kamenev and Stalin – actually supported the Provisional Government. Lenin's return changed the situation dramatically, and from April the Bolsheviks planned to overthrow the government. However, until August, 1917, all their efforts ended in complete failure. The Kornilov Affair gave the Bolsheviks the opportunity to appear as defenders of the Provisional Government against the army. As a result, they received the weapons from the Government necessary to launch a successful armed uprising. This made the Provisional Government look weak and dependant on the 'strong' Bolsheviks.

The timing of the uprising

The Bolsheviks had timed their seizure of power very cleverly. They claimed that they were acting on behalf of the Soviet – which had shared political power with the Provisional Government. Kerensky knew that the Bolsheviks were planning some kind of takeover but did not act decisively. The Bolsheviks had also organised and executed their takeover with great efficiency – and it was a virtually bloodless affair. Much of the praise for its smooth execution must go to Trotsky.

The weakness of the Provisional Government

Also, there was little support for the Provisional Government within Petrograd. The revolution had raised enormous hopes but the Provisional Government failed to tackle the most pressing issues: food shortages, inflation, the land questions, the continuation of the war. By October 1917 those failures had dramatically reduced its authority and popularity.

However, Kerensky was able to win support from some army units outside the capital. On 28 October, Cossack troops advanced on the city, and the next day, officer cadets, loyal to the Provisional Government, attempted an uprising within the city – but it was put down by the Red Guards. Finally, on the night of 30 October, a large but disorganised force of Red Guards defeated a Cossack attack at Pulkovo Heights, just outside Petrograd. These were the last attempts of the Provisional Government to regain control. From now on, it was Lenin in power.

Activity: The key to the Bolsheviks' success

Divide into small groups. Each group puts forward reasons to support one of the following as the key to the Bolsheviks' success:

- Lenin
- Trotsky's planning
- The weakness of the Provisional Government (see Chapter 9)

Report back to all the groups with a brief presentation in support of your view.

Skills Builder 3 Writing introductions and conclusions

When answering questions in Unit 1, students will be expected to write an essay.

In this third Skills Builder, we will be looking at the importance of writing introductory and concluding paragraphs.

In the exam, you should spend approximately 40 minutes on your whole essay, including:

- Planning what you are going to write
- Writing a separate paragraph for each major point you wish to make
- Checking what you have written.

Therefore, given the time constraints, you should not spend more than 5 minutes writing your introduction.

What should you put in your introduction?

Your introduction should set out what you plan to cover and discuss in your essay answer. Your introduction needs to show that you will answer the question in an analytical way – and that you haven't just started writing without thinking. Therefore, it is good to say, very briefly, what you are going to argue in the essay. You can then refer back to your introduction as you write, to make sure that your argument is on track.

We are going to look at an introduction to an answer to the following question:

> (A) How far do you agree that the main reason for the failure of the Provisional Government was the decision to continue fighting in the First World War?

This question gives one of the reasons for the failure of the Provisional Government, and it asks you 'how far' you agree that it was the most important reason. This will require you to assess other reasons why the Provisional Government failed and make judgements about the significance of each reason in bringing about the failure of the Provisional Government.

Here is an example of an introduction that you might write:

The Bolsheheviks were able to seize power from the Provisional Government in October 1917. Lasting only eight months, the Provisional Government had been faced with several problems from the very start. Although there were many reasons for the failure of the Provisional Government, such as the fact they had to share power with the Soviet, the decision to continue fighting in the First World War was the most important. Because of this they lost support from the people and, more importantly, from the armed forces, who they relied on to defend them.

This introduction shows from the beginning that the essay will focus on the question. It recognises that the Provisional Government faced a variety of problems. It refers directly to the assertion made in the question – that the decision to continue fighting in the war was the main reason for failure – and it shows that you intend to reach judgements about the statement in the essay.

It is important to link the second paragraph to the introduction. So, for this question, you could provide evidence in Paragraph 2 that supports the view that to continue fighting in the First World War was a major cause of the failure. Or you could deal with the other reasons first and build up to dealing with the main reason given in the argument – the First World War.

Introductions: Do's and Don'ts

- Do look at the question and decide what your line of argument will be.
- Do make reference to the question in your introduction.
- Do show what you intend to argue.
- Don't begin your answer by writing a story.
- Don't spend too long writing your introduction – 5 minutes is enough.

Activity: Writing your own introduction

Write an introduction to the following question:

(B) How far do you agree that Lenin's leadership was the main reason why the Bolsheviks were able to seize power in October 1917?

Why are conclusions important?

When you are asked a question in an examination, you are expected to answer it! The concluding paragraph is very important in this process. It should contain the summary of the argument you have made, with your *verdict* on the question.

Like an introduction, the conclusion should not be more than three or four sentences in length, and under examination conditions it should take no more than 5 minutes to write. Here is an example of a conclusion for Question (A):

The failure of the Provisional Government was due to a wide variety of reasons, such as poor leadership, in particular by Kerensky, and sharing power with the Soviet. However, I agree that the main reason for the failure of the Provisional Government was the decision to continue fighting in the First World War. The Provisional Government also faced very serious food shortages and inflation, both of which were made worse by the war. Defeat in the June/July offensive caused a collapse in army morale and its support for the Provisional Government, which was exploited by Lenin and the Bolsheviks. Without the support of the army the Provisional Government was weakened so much that the Bolsheviks were able to seize power in October 1917 with relative ease.

Activity: Write your own conclusion

Using the question on Lenin's leadership, Question (B) above, write a conclusion of not more than four sentences. Try to write it in 5 minutes.

Activity: Writing an introduction and a conclusion

Here is another example of a question:

(C) How far was Lenin's ability to stay in power after October 1917 due to victory in the Civil War?

Now write an introduction and a conclusion – each in approximately 5 minutes.

Tip – plan the conclusion first. You will always find it easier to write an introduction once you have decided what your conclusion will be. This is because once you know where your answer is going, you can introduce it.

Chapter 13 The consolidation of power

Key questions

- What problems did Lenin face after the October Revolution?
- What reforms did the Bolsheviks introduce when they came to power?
- Why were the Bolsheviks able to stay in power after the October Revolution?

For Lenin and the Bolsheviks, winning political power was relatively easy, compared with retaining it. The Bolsheviks may have had a temporary majority in the All-Russia Soviet in October 1917, but they did not have a majority following in the country as a whole. Russia was in chaos, politically and economically, and normal government had broken down in large areas. Yet Lenin was able to hold on to power – and create the world's first communist state.

Take note

What problems did Lenin face after the October Revolution and how did he deal with them?

The problems facing Lenin after the October Revolution

Lenin now faced enormous problems. Russia was still at war with Germany and Austria–Hungary, and occupying forces controlled most of western Russia. The Germans were only 100 miles from Petrograd. At any minute they could march on the city – which was virtually defenceless. The peasants had seized lands across the country, industrial production had slumped, unemployment was rising, and so was inflation.

Although they were strong in cities such as Petrograd and Moscow, the Bolsheviks did not have mass support across the country. Lenin felt too vulnerable at the end of October 1917 to cancel the elections to the Constituent Assembly, which took place as planned on 12 November. But the results showed clearly that the Bolsheviks had the support of only one quarter of the Russian electorate.

Forming a government

None of the Bolsheviks had any experience of governing and administration, but now Lenin and his colleagues had to form a government for the largest country on earth. The situation was made worse because government officials and employees went on strike, and the State Bank refused to release any funds to the new government.

Lenin aimed to create a government free from the control of the All-Russia Soviet. But he first ensured that the Soviet passed three decrees while the Bolsheviks held a majority. The first was the Decree on Land, which confiscated all private land and placed it in the hands of the peasants. This was one of the Bolshevik slogans before the Revolution and simply recognised what was already happening across Russia, but the decree on land showed that they were willing to compromise their principles to keep hold of power. Ultimately, the Bolsheviks wished to take all land under government control. The second decree was the Peace Decree, which took immediate steps to end the war with Germany and Austria–Hungary. The third decree set up the organisation of the new government. At the top was the Council of People's Commissars, known as 'Sovnarkom', with Lenin as chairman, equivalent to prime minister.

On 4 November, the new government began closing down newspapers which were critical of the Bolsheviks.

The government of Lenin's Russia

Sovnarkom
(Lenin was chair and most of the members were Bolsheviks)
↑
All-Russia Congress of Soviets
(The Bolsheviks held a majority)
↑
Representatives from village, city and district Soviets

Ending the war

One of the key slogans of the Bolshevik campaign in 1917 concerned 'ending the war'. Now the Bolsheviks had little choice – the war was deeply unpopular and a major contributory factor in the fall of the Provisional Government. Also, the Bolsheviks needed all their limited military resources to be used against internal enemies. An armistice (ceasefire) was agreed in December 1917, and on 22 December a Bolshevik peace delegation, led first by Alfred Joffe and then by Trotsky, began negotiations at Brest-Litovsk.

The Germans made very severe demands. They wanted to take from Russia the Baltic states of Latvia, Lithuania and Estonia, plus Poland and Ukraine. This would lead to the loss of one third of Russia's population, one third of its agricultural land and over half of its industry.

On 7 and 8 January Lenin faced a major problem in persuading his government to continue negotiations. Eventually he won his colleagues around, but the issue almost split the new government.

On 27 January Trotsky signed a peace treaty with Ukraine, and on 3 March, in the Treaty of Brest-Litovsk, the Bolsheviks ended the war with Germany officially. Russia had been forced to pay a very high price in loss of territory and economic wealth, but Lenin knew that unless he brought the war to an end, he would lose power. (In fact, once the war was over, the Bolshevik government annulled the treaty.)

Take note

1. What changes were made by the Treaty of Brest-Litovsk?
2. Why did the Constituent Assembly last for only one day?

Russian territory before and after the Treaty of Brest-Litovsk

The Constituent Assembly

The creation of a Constituent Assembly had been promised by the Provisional Government when it took over Russia after the February Revolution. Elections had been postponed on a number of occasions but were eventually promised for 12 November 1917, and took place as planned. The result was not a great surprise to Lenin. The Socialist Revolutionaries became the largest party in Russia. Lenin's main concern was how to prevent the Constituent Assembly from challenging the newly established Bolshevik rule.

The Constituent Assembly met for the first and only time on 5 January 1918 in the Tauride Palace, Petrograd. The Bolsheviks demanded that the Assembly should be subservient to decrees passed by the Soviet and Sovnarkom. This was rejected by 237 votes to 137. The Bolsheviks and Left Socialist Revolutionaries then walked out and the remaining delegates were dispersed by armed troops and Red Guards, both loyal to Lenin. This act marked the end of any hope of democracy under Lenin, and began the rule of a communist dictatorship.

The Bolsheviks were successful because the opposition was divided about what to do. In 1917–1918 the Bolshevik hold on power was very shaky, and few people at the time thought Bolshevik rule would last long. The Socialist Revolutionaries were split into two factions. The Left SRs supported the Bolsheviks and joined them in a coalition government. But the leader of the majority moderate SRs, Viktor Chernov, called for a peaceful demonstration, which was easily dispersed by Red Guards. The Mensheviks were also split between the followers of Fedor Dan and those of Julius Martov. It wasn't until May 1918 that they reunited. And by that stage Lenin was firmly in control.

Results of the National Elections to the Constituent Assembly, November 1917

Party	Percentage of the vote
Socialist Revolutionaries	40.4
Bolsheviks	24.0
Mensheviks	2.6
Left Socialist Revolutionaries	1.0
Other Socialist Parties	0.9
Kadets	4.7
Other Liberal groups	2.8
National Minorities	13.4
Others	10.2

Activity: Timeline

Construct a timeline of Lenin's rule from October 25, the Bolshevik Revolution, to 5 January 1918, the meeting of the Constituent Assembly. On the timeline identify important developments which enabled Lenin to stay in power.

Activity: Order of importance

1. Divide into small groups. Each group should place the issues listed below in order of importance to the Bolshevik consolidation of power, writing a sentence in support of each choice.
   - Forming a government
   - Ending the war
   - Giving land to the peasants
   - Closing down the Constituent Assembly.
2. Each group should then report back to the whole class. If groups have placed the issues in different orders of importance, they should defend their chosen order. At the end of the discussion see if a consensus develops about the order.

Taking it further

From information contained in this chapter, answer the following question: 'Lenin was able to consolidate his power because of the weakness of his opponents.' Can you identify evidence to support OR refute this view?

Chapter 14 The Civil War

Key questions

- Why did Civil War break out?
- How did the Civil War develop?
- Why did the Bolsheviks* win the Civil War?

* Note that the Bolsheviks were renamed 'Communists' in early 1918.

The greatest challenge facing Lenin after he took power was the outbreak of the Civil War, in which more Russians died than in the First World War. The Civil War was fought right across Russia and involved several different forces. The Reds were the defenders of Lenin and his revolution. The Whites were a loose collection of anti-Red forces, most of which wanted a return to a Tsarist-type regime. The Greens were opponents of both the Reds and the Whites and supported a radical alternative to communist government. The Greens wanted political and economic power handed to local groups of peasants. Nationalists, such as Finns, Poles, Ukrainians and Georgians, fought for national independence. Finally, several foreign states, such as Britain, France, the USA and Japan, sent troops to Russia to fight alongside the Whites.

Given the range of military forces against him, it seems surprising that Lenin and his government were able to survive. However, by 1921, Lenin had won the Civil War – and Communist rule was firmly established.

The outbreak of Civil War, 1918

It is difficult to find a precise event that led to the outbreak of war. Some historians have cited the October Revolution itself as the start. Others have seen the beginning of the conflict as a general deterioration in law and order as the Communists established their control during early 1918. What is true is that by the spring of 1918 Lenin's government was involved in a major conflict with a variety of different enemies. What all the enemies had in common was a desire to remove Lenin and his government.

First, there were counter-revolutionary forces that wanted a return to the days of the Tsar and/or the Provisional Government. This was a loose and diverse group, ranging from monarchists to liberals. These were termed the 'White' forces. They began forming under the leadership of General Kornilov, but after his death in April 1918 they came under the control of General Deniken and numbered approximately 19,000. This group was based in southern Russia. In the Baltic region, near Petrograd, another White, General Yudenich, amassed a force in order to retake Petrograd. Due to fears of both White and German attack, Lenin moved his capital to Moscow in early 1918. Finally, in Siberia, under Admiral Kolchak, White forces established their own government.

In an attempt to keep Russia in the First World War, Allied countries sent expeditionary forces to fight with the White armies. The British sent forces to Murmansk and Archangel in North Russia, the French occupied Odessa on the Black Sea, and the Japanese took over Vladivostok on the Pacific Ocean. Although the First World War was coming to a close by the end of summer 1918, these forces remained in Russia. With revolutionary outbreaks in Germany and Hungary, many European powers saw Communist Russia as a threat to stability in their own countries and stayed on to help the Whites try to overthrow Lenin and his revolutionary government.

Military opposition to the Communists

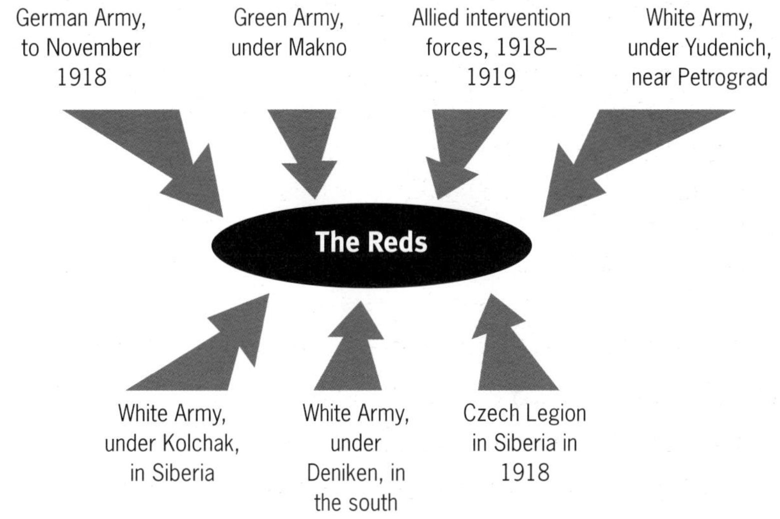

The First World War also created another strange development, involving the Czech Legion. This group was created in 1917 out of Austro-Hungarian prisoners of war of Czech and Slovak origin who wanted to create their own national state. In 1918 the Legion, which by now comprised 40,000 troops, attempted to make its way west from Siberia across Russia, using the Trans-Siberian railway. It intended to become involved in the war against Germany, but as it moved westward it came into conflict with Red forces. As the Czech Legion neared the western Siberian town of Ekaterinburg, the Communist forces there, who were holding the former Tsar and his family prisoners, executed them, rather than see them fall into the hands of the approaching Czechs.

Take note

Identify the various reasons why the Bolsheviks faced so much opposition in 1918.

Another factor in causing civil war was the desire of many nationalities to form their own states. Finns fought for their independence, as did Poles, Ukrainians and the peoples of the Caucasus region. (It is interesting to note that the Communists themselves had many leaders of non-Russian origin. Lenin was part German and part Kalmyk, Stalin was a Georgian, and Trotsky, Kamenev and Zinoviev were Jewish.)

Take note

What were the major successes and failures of the Red Army in the Civil War period?

Opponents of the Communists

Opponent	Reason
Allied Intervention Forces in 1918	• To overthrow the Communists and get Russia back in the First World War
White Armies	Different reasons: • To return Russia to rule by a monarchy (the majority of Whites wanted this) • To establish democratic rule
Green Armies	• To create a society based on local organisations of peasants
Left SRs	• To create a more open society with major social and economic change to aid the peasants • Opposition to the Treaty of Brest-Litovsk
Nationalist movements	• To gain independence from Russian rule

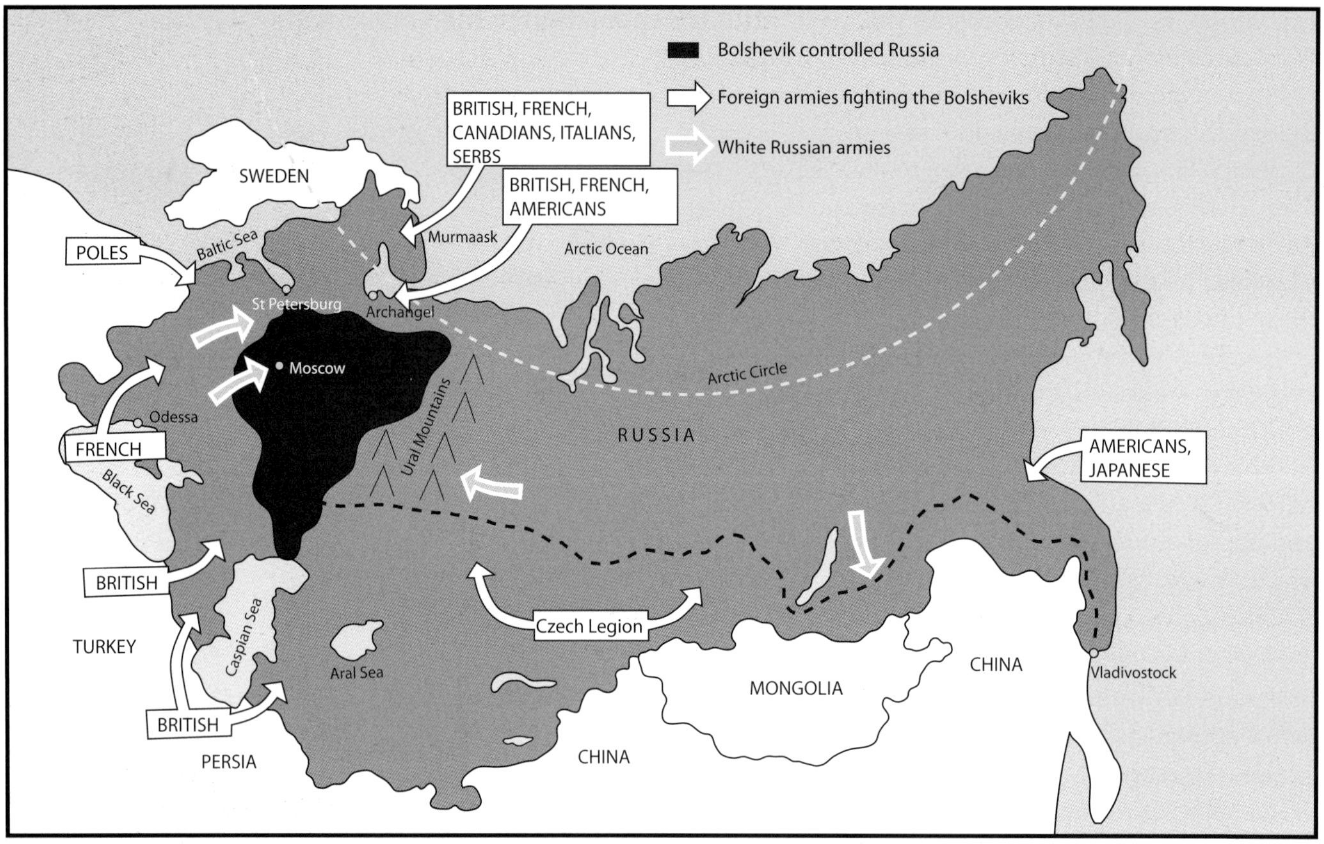

The Russian Civil War and foreign intervention 1918–1921

Take note

What were the reasons for Communist success in the Civil War?

Finally, the unpopular and humiliating Treaty of Brest-Litovsk in March 1918 caused a split with the Left Social Revolutionaries, who were the coalition partners of the Communists. In June 1918 the Left SRs launched an attack on Communist rule, with Lenin himself suffering an assassination attempt. The Left SRs also assassinated the German ambassador, von Mirbach, in the hope of forcing the Germans to intervene to topple the Communists. The Left SRs, however, were defeated by the Red Army.

The crucial year – 1919

The war went through a series of phases, but the big turning points came mainly in 1919. At several points in this year the Communists almost lost major battles, but managed to repulse the Whites at the last minute.

Kolchak's campaign – the East

At the beginning of the year, Admiral Kolchak launched an assault from the East. Kolchak had the support of 30,000 foreign troops and initially the offensive went well. By April, his armies had advanced 200 miles and captured some important cities. However, at the end of April the Red Army launched a counterattack, conscripting civilians into the Red Army and persuading some of Kolchak's forces to change sides. By July Kolchak's forces had been pushed back to where they started from and lost most of their men.

Deniken's campaign – the South-East

General Deniken's army was based in South East Russia. Initially he agreed to help Kolchak's campaign, but in March he changed his mind and went to the Donbass region to fight the Red Army who had just invaded the area. At first he had some success and many people deserted from the Red Army as it retreated. But he did not have enough troops to fight over such a large front, and eventually his attack failed.

Yudenich's campaign – Petrograd

Yudenich launched an attack against Communist-controlled Petrograd in October 1919. He badly needed more men, but foreign support had dried up following Kolchak's retreat and the Finns refused to fight with him as he wouldn't promise to grant them independence from Russia if they won. Despite this, Yudenich's attack got off to a good start, but Trotsky intervened, rousing troops and workers in Petrograd and personally rounding up retreating troops to lead them into battle, securing victory for the Communists.

In the face of so many defeats, the foreign powers became disheartened and by the end of 1919, the vast majority of foreign troops had been withdrawn and the Czech Legion had left Russia. Without foreign support, the White armies went into headlong retreat. By 1920 the last major White army, under General Wrangel, was cornered on the Crimean peninsula in southern Russia, and it was destroyed by a Communist offensive by the middle of 1920.

The Russo-Polish War, 1920–1921

When Lenin took power in October 1917 he saw the takeover as the start of a worldwide Communist revolution. Russia was merely the first country to fall to this new social order. During the Civil War, Lenin made one unsuccessful attempt to spread the revolution westwards.

In 1919, exploiting the chaotic conditions of the Russian Civil War, Polish forces had entered western Ukraine and captured Kiev, the capital. The Communists attacked and forced the Poles to retreat. Lenin then ordered the invasion of Poland as the prelude to a war against central Europe. He hoped that Polish workers would join the Red Army and stage a revolution against their government, but in fact they saw the Russians as a foreign aggressor and fought against them. In 1920 the Red Army managed to get to the gates of Warsaw, the Polish capital, before being defeated. At the subsequent Treaty of Riga, in April 1921, Poland was given a large part of western Belorussia. The Russo-Polish War constituted the biggest Communist defeat in the Civil War and ended any attempt by Lenin to extend the Revolution beyond Russia.

Reasons for the Communist victory

Given the diverse forces massed against them, it might seem surprising that the Communists won the war. Their success was due in part to their own skill and organisation of their forces and also in part to the failures of their opponents.

Anton Deniken

(1872–1947)

General who served in the Russo-Japanese War and the First World War. He took part in the Kornilov Affair against the Bolsheviks in August 1917. After the October Revolution he organised White armies in south east Russia. But he failed to co-operate with other White generals, which helped result in his own defeat.

Cheka

This was the name of the terror police force created by Lenin on 6 December 1917. In Russian, CHEKA stood for the All-Russia Extraordinary Commission for the Suppression of Counter Revolution and Sabotage. This was a major departure from the policies of the Provisional Government which had abolished the Okhrana (the Tsarist secret police) and the death penalty.
The Cheka's main purpose was to arrest, imprison and execute political opponents. It also ran a concentration camp system called the 'Gulag'. The Cheka existed from December 1917 to February 1922. In 1971 the British historian Robert Conquest claimed that it had been responsible for 500,000 deaths.

Admiral Kolchak

(1873–1920)

Admiral who served in the Russian navy in the Russo-Japanese War and the First World War. In the Civil War he formed a White government in the Far East and then a White government in Siberia, based on the city of Omsk, where he declared himself 'Supreme Ruler' of Russia. He was captured by the Czech Legion and handed over to the Communists, who executed him in 1920.

Nikolai Yudenich

(1862–1933)

A highly successful general in the First World War, where he won several victories over the Ottoman Turks, on the Caucasus Front. He commanded the White Forces on the north-western Front and made an unsuccessful attack on Petrograd in 1919.

The disunity of the opposition

The Communists had a strong central leadership under Lenin. He had the vision and the determination to lead the government through the years of crisis. The Communists were united and well-organised with the ruthless determination needed to win. By contrast anti-Communist forces lacked a clear strategy or central direction of their war effort. The White forces fought for different reasons: many fought to re-establish tsarism, some were liberals who favoured a return to the Provisional Government. This lack of unity made it difficult to win the hearts and minds of ordinary Russians, most of whom did not want a return to tsarism.

In addition, some anti-communists forces fought amongst themselves, weakening their chances of defeating the Communists. Ukrainian nationalists, for example, fought both White and Red armies. A Green Army was formed under Nestor Makhno. The Greens wanted to create a new type of society where political and economic control was in the hands of local groups of peasants. Makhno operated successfully against the Communists in 1918, only to be defeated by the Red Army in 1919.

Geographical and organisational factors

The Communists dominated the heartland of Russia – an area between Petrograd, Moscow and Tsaritsyn (now Volgograd) with a population of approximately 60 million. Moscow and Petrograd were important industrial centres and the area also included most of Russia's railway network. This territory was continuous and unbroken by areas under opposition control. This was a huge advantage to the Communists for the following reasons:

- They could produce more munitions than the White armies, who had to rely on foreign support.
- They could use the railways to distribute munitions to the various Fronts.
- They could use the railways to quickly send troops to wherever they were needed.
- They could communicate more effectively because their territory was continuous, allowing them to coordinate attacks against their enemies.

By contrast, the Whites were geographically dispersed. In addition, White generals launched offensives at different times, allowing Red forces to move around and defeat them one by one.

The Communists were also extremely efficient and well coordinated in their approach to the war. The Communists were also able to maximise the production of weapons through the introduction of War Communism. Under this economic system the Communists conscripted people to work in factories and used coercive tactics, such as fear of imprisonment, to force workers to produce more weapons. The Communists took over war production and centrally controlled all economic activity. Groups of elite workers were sent round the various economic sectors to deal with bottlenecks in production. Crucially, they were able to feed the cities through 'grain requisitioning' – taking grain from peasants by force. This was not popular with peasants, and may have contributed to the popularity of the Green forces, but was critically important for the war effort.

The Terror

To remove any form of political opposition, Lenin established the Cheka, a political police force that engaged in terror tactics against all enemies of the Communists. Terror tactics were used against anyone who resisted the Communists in any way. For example, peasants who tried to resist grain requisitioning were executed and villages thought to be hiding political opponents were burned. Many civilians and would-be opponents were offered the choice between joining the Red Army or execution.

Trotsky addressing troops during the Civil War, 1920

Trotsky and the Red Army

Another important factor in Communist success was the military leadership of Leon Trotsky. In 1918 Trotsky founded the Red Army, which by the end of the Civil War in 1921 had reached 5 million in number, many of whom were conscripted. Trotsky was faced with a dilemma: the Communists lacked members with high-level military experience. In response to this, he introduced the controversial policy of recruiting former officers of the Tsarist army to fight for the Communists. But Trotsky was clever. To ensure their loyalty he held their families hostage. In addition, political officers were assigned to all Red Army units to ensure that they complied with Trotsky's orders and remained loyal to the Communists. In addition, he himself toured every Front in the war in an armoured train, checking up on his units and delivering stirring political speeches. Together, these measures ensured that the Red Army fought effectively.

Activity: What did they do in the Civil War?

Divide into small groups. Each group should explain the role of one of the following in the Civil War and report its findings back to the whole class:

- Lenin
- The Cheka
- Trotsky
- White generals
- The Poles

Then, individually, write down the most important reason why the Communists won the Civil War, giving reasons to support your answer.

Taking it further

Answer the following question from information contained within this chapter:
'The Communists won the Civil War mainly because of the weaknesses of their opponents.' Assess this view.

Chapter 15 War Communism

Key questions

- How did Lenin try to introduce communism to Russia?
- What was War Communism?
- Why was War Communism abandoned in 1921?

When Lenin took power in October 1917 he was a man on a mission. He planned to create a type of society and economy which had never appeared before – the world's first communist state. In doing so, he was engaging in the world's greatest social and economic experiment. Not only did Lenin want to transform the country, he attempted to do so at a time of enormous political instability, civil war and economic decline. The results of this social and economic experimentation took Lenin's state to the point of collapse by 1921.

Take note

How did Lenin attempt to introduce a communist-style economy between December 1917 and June 1918?

Take note

What were the main features of War Communism?

What did Lenin do to transform the society and economy in 1917–1918?

Lenin's aim was nothing short of a complete replacement of the capitalist economic system by communism. On 2 December 1917, Lenin created the Supreme Council of National Economy (the Vesenkha) to offer central control of the Russian economy. On 14 December the army was used to take over all the banks, which were then declared to be owned by the Communist Government. On 21 January 1918 Lenin caused international uproar by declaring that all foreign debts incurred by the Tsar and Provisional Government were illegal and would not be paid. Under the new regime, all landowners lost their estates. Even money itself was abolished at one stage.

In this period, from December 1917 to June 1918, Russia experienced what historians have called 'State capitalism', which recognised workers' control of their factories. Workers took control of factories and set their own hours of work and the level of production. Industrial production slumped, however, and the economy operated mainly on a barter system, where shortages in essential goods produced a flourishing black market. By June 1918 Lenin's government was also faced with a Civil War, where it had to fight for its very existence. If the Bolsheviks were to wage war successfully they needed to have enough food to feed the army and they would also need to produce enough guns and ammunition to defeat their opponents. The whole economy needed to be geared towards these ends. This situation forced Lenin to introduce a new economic policy – 'War Communism'.

What was War Communism?

- A Supreme Economic Council was formed to run the economy.
- Nationalisation of industry. The Decree on Nationalisation in the summer of 1918 made all large industries liable to nationalisation without compensation. By 1920 around 37,000 businesses had been nationalised.

- Private trade was banned.
- Grain surpluses were seized from peasants. Anyone caught withholding grain was liable to be shot.
- A steep decline in the use of money. This was replaced by rationing organised by the state.
- The use of terror, slave labour and seizure of goods and grain by the state.

The result was chaotic. The political commissars who were responsible for War Communism found it impossible to completely eliminate the free market. Rations were completely inadequate and the black market flourished.

The whole of the Russian economy that was under Communist control was organised on a war footing. The Commissariat of Supplies (Narkomprod) made sure that rations were given to workers on the basis of their output and the importance of their work. The towns and cities were fed by the 'Ural–Siberian method' of grain requisitioning, in which groups of committed Communists were sent into the countryside to requisition (seize) grain from peasants.

Take note

In what ways was War Communism a success and in what ways was it a failure?

What impact did War Communism have on Russia?

On the one hand, War Communism allowed the Communists to win the Civil War. It allowed Lenin's government to concentrate on the production of weapons and military equipment. On the other, this was only achieved at great human cost.

Between 1917 and 1920 over half of the urban working population disappeared – and this was the class on which Lenin had hoped to build his new socialist society Their decline was due to a number of factors, such as death in the Civil War, famine or going back to their villages to find food. Partly as a result of War Communism and partly as a result of the Civil War, Russia suffered a major famine in 1921. Peasants stopped producing so much grain when they realised it was going to be taken from them. This, combined with the disruption of the war and drought, caused the famine which resulted in the death of between one and two million people. Peasants were extremely resentful of grain requisitioning, and peasant uprisings occurred right across Russia. One of the worst, in Tambov province in 1920–1921, helped force Lenin to reappraise his economic policy. War Communism also failed to stop the fall in industrial production. As a result, at the Tenth Party Congress of the Communist Party in 1921, Lenin announced the end of War Communism.

Starving children during the Russian famine of 1921.

Timeline

1917	October: Bolshevik seizure of power December: Creation of Vesenkha; nationalisation of the banks
1918	January: Lenin cancels all foreign and domestic debts June: Introduction of War Communism
1920	Peasant rebellions against grain requisitioning
1921	Lenin abandons War Communism Famine in Russia

Activity: Source analysis: War Communism

Study the four sources below, and answer the following questions:

1. How do Sources B and C differ in their view of War Communism?
2. Considering all the sources, what evidence is there to suggest that War Communism was a failure?

Source A: Industrial production compared, 1913 and 1921

	1913	***1921***
Coal (million tonnes)	29	9
Oil (million tonnes)	9	4
Electricity (million Kwh)	2039	520
Pig iron (million tonnes)	4.2	0.1
Steel (million tonnes)	4.3	0.2
Bricks (millions)	2.1	0.01

Source B: Lenin on War Communism in 1921

'War Communism was imposed by war and ruin. It was not and could not be a policy that corresponded to the economic tasks of the industrial working class. It was a temporary measure.'

Source C: Trotsky, writing in 1928, on War Communism

'War Communism in its original form pursued broad aims. The Soviet Government hoped and strove to develop these methods of regimentation directly into a system of planned economy in distribution as well as production. In other words, from War Communism it hoped gradually to arrive at genuine communism.'

Source D: American historian Richard Pipes, writing in The Russian Revolution, Vintage Books USA, 1991

'Under War Communism the Bolsheviks had been living off the human and material resources accumulated by pre-1917 Russia. But there was a limit to those. An analysis published in the summer of 1920 in the leading Soviet economic newspaper concluded, "We have completely exhausted the supplies of the more important resources and raw materials bequeathed to us by capitalist Russia."'

Chapter 16 The New Economic Policy

Key questions

- Why was the New Economic Policy introduced in 1921?
- What were the main features of the New Economic Policy?
- What impact did the New Economic Policy have on Russia by the time of Lenin's death?

At the beginning of 1921 the White forces had been defeated and the Communists had won the Civil War. Lenin's regime, which had come to power in very precarious circumstances in October 1917, had survived more than three years. Yet Lenin was facing a major crisis at the beginning of 1921. Russia had serious economic problems. World War, revolution and Civil War had ravaged the country – millions had died, thousands of villages had been destroyed and industrial production had plummeted. For the Communist regime to survive, Lenin had to consider major changes in how the economy performed and how the government of Russia was to be organised.

The introduction of the New Economic Policy

The economic situation

By early 1921 the Russian economy seemed to be in meltdown. Industrial production was a fraction of pre-First World War levels. War Communism and its policy of requisitioning grain had led to peasant uprisings across Russia. The Tambov Uprising had been so serious that large forces of the Red Army had to be diverted to the province to restore law and order. The Communist Government seemed to be at war with the majority of the Russian population – the peasantry. To make matters even worse, the first signs of a major famine were appearing.

Take note

Identify reasons why Lenin decided to introduce the New Economic Policy in 1921.

Growing opposition

These developments caused unease among Communist Party members. They were concerned about the increasing central control exercised by Lenin's government. In particular, there was considerable unease about Trotsky's 'solution' to the economic crisis – his plan to extend compulsory service beyond the Red Army to include the civilian work force as well. By the end of 1920 the Mensheviks began increasing their support in local soviets. At the same time, a Workers' Opposition movement was developing, based on disapproval of the government's control of the trade unions.

The Kronstadt Rebellion, March 1921

When Lenin took power in October 1917, one of his most loyal supporters was the naval base at Kronstadt, near Petrograd. This was the home of the Revolutionary Baltic Fleet whose sailors had participated in the takeover of 25 October 1917 and in the Civil War. However, this group had now become completely disillusioned with Lenin's rule. And by March 1921 a large proportion of the Kronstadt sailors were conscripted Ukrainians rather than the men who had assisted Lenin into power in 1917. None of them were happy with the situation and they demanded an end to the special position of the Communist Party, a relaxation of economic controls and the restoration of freedom of speech.

Their demands led directly to an open rebellion against Lenin's regime, and Trotsky was given the task of putting it down. Using elite troops of the Red Army, he attacked the naval base, which was on an island in the Gulf of Finland, by crossing the frozen sea. Over three weeks, the rebellion was put down, with great ferocity, and those rebels who were not killed were sent to the gulags which were forced labour camps.

The Tenth Party Congress, March 1921

Take note

What were the main decisions taken by the Tenth Party Congress?

The Kronstadt Rebellion, together with all the other problems mentioned above, meant that the Tenth meeting of the Communist Party, held at the end of March 1921, was always going to be a significant event. But Lenin astonished most of the delegates by his announcements. First, and most importantly, he announced the end of War Communism. He said that it had been only a temporary measure, brought on by the needs of the Civil War, and it would now be replaced by a 'New Economic Policy'. Under this new policy, the requisitioning of foodstuffs was abandoned. Instead, the peasants only had to give part of their produce to the government, and the rest could be sold on the open market – and the peasants had to pay a tax .

To increase the availability of goods, private trading was allowed. This led to the growth of a new class – the 'Nepmen' – private traders who were able to buy and sell goods. By 1922, only one year after the introduction of the New Economic Policy (NEP), nearly three-quarters of all trade was conducted by this new group. To assist these economic changes, a new currency was introduced in 1922, which helped bring an end to the high level of inflation (rising prices).

Lenin announced that his plan was a 'tactical retreat' in order to preserve Communist power, and that what he was doing was giving the Russian economy a 'breathing space'. Despite these changes, the majority of workers still worked in state-run enterprises, and the government kept under its control what it called 'the commanding heights of the economy' – banking, heavy industry, transportation and foreign trade.

'Democratic centralism' and the ban on internal factions

The NEP was a radical departure. To many Communists it was a betrayal of their ideas, and Lenin was acutely aware that it could split the Party. He had already experienced the intense debate within the Party over the signing of the Treaty of Brest-Litovsk in 1918. To prevent this level of discord happening again, Lenin announced a ban on factions within the Communist Party. Party members, therefore, were no longer allowed to form groups independent from Lenin's leadership. This ban would be supplemented by the idea of 'democratic centralism'. From now on, decisions made by Lenin and the

Politburo would be binding on all other Communists – and all other political parties were banned.

The introduction of the NEP, therefore, saw a loosening of economic controls but a tightening of political control. From March 1921, Russia was governed by a dictatorship more absolute than any government under the Tsarist autocracy.

Glossary: Politburo

The main decision-making committee of the Communist Party.

The impact of the NEP on the Russian economy

The NEP had an almost immediate effect. Markets returned to Russian towns and cities, more goods became available, food shortages disappeared and the famine of 1921 came to an end. By 1923, 85 per cent of firms were again in private hands. Peasants began cultivating more land – the area of land under cultivation rising by half between 1921 and 1927 – and numbers of livestock increased. Coal and textile production doubled over the same period.

Take note

How did the Russian economy change after the introduction of the NEP?

But the impact of the NEP was not all positive. It helped spark off what was called the 'Scissors Crisis' – the ever-widening gap between agricultural prices and industrial prices. As agricultural production rose, the price of agricultural goods fell. Meanwhile, industrial prices rose, because of shortages. Therefore, peasants – the majority of the population – had to pay more and more for manufactured goods at a time when they were getting less and less for their produce. (The problem was called the 'Scissors Crisis' because the gap in prices was said to resemble the widening blades of a pair of scissors when opened.)

The NEP was also accused by many Communists of encouraging greed, independence and self-interest. For this group, the shorter the NEP lasted, the better. By the time of Lenin's death in 1924, the debate over the future of the NEP was becoming a serious issue in the Communist Party.

Smolensk Market in Moscow during the NEP period.

Activity: The arguments about the NEP

You are a member of the Communist Party attending the Tenth Party Congress in March 1921. Write a report of the arguments you heard which supported and opposed the introduction of the New Economic Policy. In your report make reference to the consequences of introducing the NEP, such as the ban on internal factions, democratic centralism, and the ban on all other political parties.

Taking it further

Study Chapter 15 on War Communism and this chapter on the New Economic Policy. Draw up a list of similarities and differences between the two policies.

Chapter 17 The creation of the USSR

Key questions

- Why did Lenin create the USSR?
- Was Lenin a Red Tsar?
- How had Russia changed from 1917 to 1924?

By 1922 Lenin had given up the immediate prospect of worldwide Communist Revolution. His attempt to spread revolution westward had ended with defeat in the Russo-Polish War. Also, in introducing the New Economic Policy, Lenin had had to make a tactical retreat on the introduction of communism within Russia. In attempting to keep power, he had reduced government control of the economy but, in contrast, had increased dictatorial control of the political system. Now, an important issue with which Lenin had to deal was how to build a new state, made up of different nationalities.

The creation of the USSR, 1922

Take note

How did the creation of the USSR change the way Russia was governed?

On 29 December 1922 Lenin oversaw the creation of a new state: the Union of Soviet Socialist Republics (USSR). The new state would comprise the Russian Soviet Federative Socialist Republic (RSFSR), the Ukrainian Social Republic, the Belorussian Soviet Socialist Republic and the Transcaucasian Soviet Socialist Republic. This new state still contained the aspiration of worldwide revolution. The USSR was the only state without a geographical limitation in its name (and by 1945 it would comprise fifteen republics).

Until 1921 Lenin ruled the area called the RSFSR. By the end of the Civil War the Communists had extended their rule over much of the old Russian Empire. However, in the Peace Treaties after the First World War Russia had lost control of Finland, Poland and the Baltic States. Yet the territory left under Communist control was still made up of many nationalities. The creation of the USSR was Lenin's solution of creating a multi-national Communist state, in which each republic would possess its own government, as part of a federal structure. At federal level, the individual republics would send representatives to a Congress of Republics which, with the Congress of Soviets, constituted the national parliament of the USSR.

Lenin's dictatorship

Take note

What were the main features of Lenin's dictatorship?

Even though the USSR was a federal state, political power was firmly in the hands of the Communist Party. From 1921 no other political parties were allowed in the USSR. Only Communists could stand for the Soviets so, in reality, the Communist Party controlled the government. The most senior committee of the USSR was the Council of People's Commissars (Sovnarkom). However, the main policy-making body of the USSR was the Politburo, the senior committee of the Communist Party.

By the time of his first serious illness, in 1922, Lenin ruled Russia in a way that would be the envy of any Tsar. He possessed complete control over the Communist Party and Government. As the founder of the Bolshevik/Communist Party – and its major political thinker – he had enormous prestige. And Communist propaganda effectively exploited Lenin as the father of the nation. From 1921 the doctrine of democratic centralism ensured that decisions made by Lenin and the Politburo would be followed by the entire Party.

Lenin also controlled the media. Only Communist newspapers, such as *Pravda*, were allowed, so the Russian people were told what Lenin wanted them to hear. In order to prevent any opposition, in 1917 Lenin had established a terror police force, the Cheka. In 1922 the Cheka was dissolved, only to be replaced by the GPU (State Political Administration), another political police force. In September 1918 Lenin had also been responsible for the introduction of the gulag system of labour camps, built to contain opponents of the regime. By the time of Lenin's death in 1924, the Gulag had imprisoned tens of thousands of victims.

Lenin's control over the USSR, therefore, was virtually total – he had created the world's first totalitarian dictatorship.

Glossary:

Belorussian SSR

The modern-day state of Belarus.

Transcaucasian SSR

Comprised the modern-day states of Georgia, Armenia and Azerbaijan.

Federal state

A political structure where political power is split between a central (federal) government and individual state governments. In the case of the USSR, the whole structure was controlled by the Communist Party.

Activity: From autocracy to dictatorship

1. **Timeline** Construct a timeline from 1881 to 1924, and on it locate what you regard as the ten most important events in the history of Russia. Which of the events that you identified helped to modernise Russia?
2. **Making comparisons** From the information contained within this book, you should now be able to make a comparison between Russia under the Tsars, Russia under the Provisional Government, and Communist Russia. Using the framework below, write down a brief description of how each type of regime was organised, and then answer the questions below.

	Tsarist Russia	Provisional Government	Communist Russia
The power of the Government			
The role of the police	The Okhrana, secret police		The Cheka and the GPU
Control over the economy			
Treatment of national minorities			The creation of the USSR
The development of political parties			

(a) Describe how the government of Russia changed in the period 1881 to 1924.

(b) How different was life in Communist Russia from life in Tsarist Russia?

(c) Can you identify any difference between Tsarist autocracy and Communist dictatorship?

Taking it further

Write an essay entitled: 'How far had Russia changed in the period 1881 to 1924?'

Skills Builder 4: **Extended writing**

So far, in the Skills Builders, you have learned about:

- The importance of writing in paragraphs
- Answering questions on causation and change
- How to write introductions and conclusions.

Now you are going to learn about how to write a full response to an examination question. Remember, you will only have 40 minutes for each answer so you need to make the most of your time.

Read the QUESTION PAPER thoroughly

You will have a choice of two questions on this topic, but you only need to answer one. Make sure that you make the right choice. Don't rush. Allow time – a few minutes – to decide on which question to answer. You won't have time to change your mind halfway through the exam.

Read YOUR CHOSEN QUESTION thoroughly

Once you have made your choice, examine the question to see what you are expected to do.

What is the question asking you to do?

There are a number of different types of question you could be asked. Each one will require you to write an answer which contains clear analysis of the question in a particular way. Examples of different types of questions are:

- How far do you agree that...?
- How important was...?
- To what extent...?
- Why...?

In the first three question types, you will be expected to organise your factual knowledge and understanding of a topic into a 'For' versus 'Against' format, where you weigh up the importance of each factor/reason/ point you mention in relation to the question. You will need to reach a judgement on the question in hand. The fourth type, a question beginning 'Why', will expect you to show how factors combined to bring about an outcome.

In your planning you also need to be clear about the focus of the question. For example, is it asking you to assess the reasons for something, the result of something or the extent to which something changed? For instance:

(A) How far was the First World War the main cause of the fall of the Romanovs in February 1917?

(B) How far was the Communist dictatorship under Lenin different from Tsarist autocracy in the reign of Alexander III?

Both these questions begin 'How far...?' but their focus is different. (A) asks you for an assessment of which cause was most important, while (B) asks you for an assessment of similarity and difference. You could usefully look at the questions for other options in Unit 1 and get some practice at recognising the focus of questions. They could also be asking for an assessment of consequences or an analysis of key features. This will help you plan so as to focus your information on what the question wants from you.

Make a plan

Once you have decided what question to answer, sketch out what you intend to cover. Write down what you think will be relevant information in the form of a list. Then organise your information in a way which best answers the question.

Writing the answer

Make sure that you:

- Write a brief introductory paragraph, setting out what you will be discussing in your answer
- Write a separate paragraph for each factor/reason you give. In the paragraph, make sure that you provide a reason which is supported by factual knowledge
- Avoid just writing descriptions
- Avoid merely 'telling a story'
- Write a concluding paragraph which sums up your arguments and provides a clear judgement on the question.

Pace yourself

Success in an examination is based partly on effective time management. If you have approximately 40 minutes to answer a question, make sure that after about 12 or 13 minutes you have written about one third of your answer. And after 35 minutes you should be thinking about and then writing your conclusion.

If you run short of time, make sure that you can still write a proper concluding paragraph. If necessary, you can save time by cutting short your treatment of the paragraph or paragraphs before, by:

- Writing the first sentence containing your point
- Bullet-pointing your evidence for this point – the information that backs it up
- Writing the last sentence of the paragraph which explains the linkage of your point to the question.

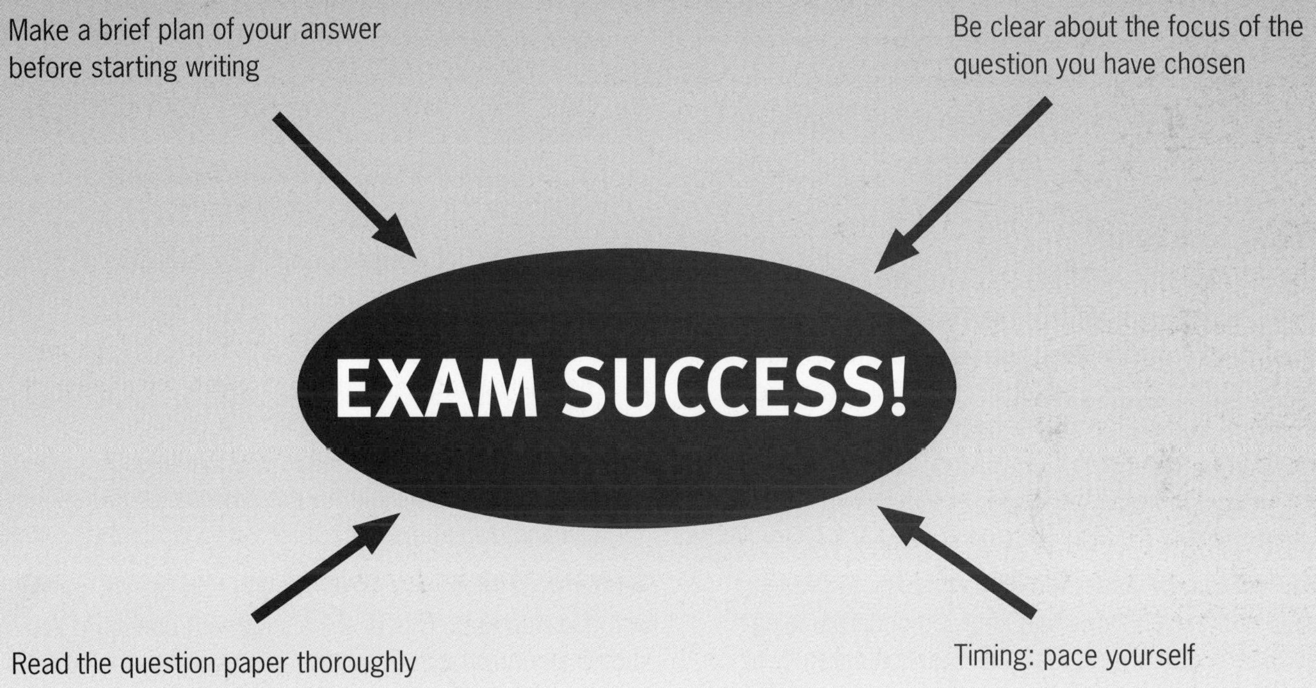

Activity: Write your own answer

Now write your own answer to the following question, following the guidance given above.

(C) How far do you agree that the main reason why the Bolsheviks stayed in power from October 1917 to 1921 was their victory in the Civil War?

Examzone

Now that you have finished the course content, you will have to do the last bits of preparation for the exam itself. This advice covers two important elements for exam success: revising the information and using your information well in the examination

This topic – 'Russia in Revolution, 1881–1924: From Autocracy to Dictatorship'– is part of Edexcel's Option D: A World Divided: Communism and Democracy in the 20th Century, in Unit 1. The Unit 1 exam will be 1 hour and 20 minutes in length, and is worth 60 marks in total.

In the exam you will be given the choice of two questions on the topic Russia in Revolution. You will be expected to answer one of these and should spend no more than half the examination time answering it. You will also have to answer another question from a different topic. You will be expected to answer the questions you choose in essay form.

What to expect

You will need to remember information, but the exam is mainly testing whether or not you can apply the relevant information in answering a question. You will be assessed on your ability to recall and select historical knowledge and to deploy it (i.e. make use of knowledge to support your points). You can see that it's not just knowing what happened which counts, but understanding how to use what you know.

You will also be assessed on your ability to present historical explanations that show an understanding of history. You should read the question carefully to make sure you answer it in the right way. Sometimes questions will simply begin 'Why'. These are asking you to analyse the causes of an event or development. For the highest marks you will need to show how factors combined to bring about the event.

Most questions will ask you for a judgment. Here are some different types of question stems you may come across in the exam:

1 How far was x responsible for y?
2 To what extent did x change?
3 How far did x depend on y?
4 Did x play a major part in y?

Although judgment questions come in a variety of forms, they are all asking you to balance points. In the case of example 2 below, you will be looking for evidence of change and of continuity in order to reach a judgment about the extent of change.

When you choose your question in the examination, take note of what sort of judgment it asks you to make. The essay questions test a variety of skills. Here are some examples of different skills being tested by the questions.

- The analysis of, and judgment about, the **key features** of a situation.
  For example: *How extensive was opposition to Nicholas II in the years 1894 to 1914?*
- The analysis of, and judgment about, the extent of **change**.
  For example: *How far did Witte improve and modernise the Russian economy?*
- The analysis of **consequences or effects**.
  For example: *How far did the 1905 Revolution affect the way in which Russia was governed?*
- The analysis of, and judgment about, the causes of a historical event or situation.
  For example: *To what extent was Nicholas II personally responsible for the downfall of the Romanovs in February 1917?*

Another type of question will ask you how far you agree with a statement,. This is still a judgment question. You should clarify what the statement is about so that you know what the question expects of you:

- Is a statement about causation, like this question: *How far do you agree that the Bolsheviks won the Civil War of 1918–1921 because they controlled more people and had access to more weapons?*
- Or is it about consequence, like this question: *How far do you agree that the 1905 Revolution had little effect on the way Russia was governed in the years to 1914?*

When you are clear about what the question wants from you, you can use what you have learned in the skills builder sections of this book to produce an answer based on extended writing (an essay) which will help you to gain high marks.

How to revise

Make a revision plan

Before you start revising, make a plan. Otherwise it is easy to waste your precious revision time. It is helpful to look at your exam dates and work backwards to the first date you intend to start revising. Here are some tips on how to create a revision plan:

1. First, fill in the dates of your examinations and then any regular commitments you have. This will help give you a realistic idea of how much time you have to revise.
2. Plan your time carefully, assigning more time to topics you find difficult.
3. Use a revision 'checklist'. Look at what you need to know and try to identify any gaps in your knowledge.
4. Now fill in the timetable with sensible work slots and breaks.
5. Keep to this timetable! Organise yourself well and it will help you to fulfill your potential. If you have not prepared a revision plan yet, it is not too late to start. Put your plan up somewhere visible so you can refer back to it.

Revision tips

- Revise often – try to do a little every day.
- Make sure you have one day a week when you don't do revision or even think about exams – you'll come back to it refreshed.
- Take a 5- or 10-minute break every hour, and do some stretching exercises, go for a short walk or make a drink.
- Talk to your family or a friend about your revision – they may be able to help you. For example, they could test you on key facts.
- Keep bullet points on 'crib cards' highlighting important revision points. For example, you could have a list or a mind map of the reasons why the Communists won the Civil War. Use these for quick revision and for reading during 'dead' times – when you're waiting for a bus, for example.
- Use mnemonics. This is when you take the first letter of a series of words you want to remember and then make a new sentence. A common mnemonic for remembering the order of the points of the compass (North, East, South, and West) is 'Naughty Elephants Squirt Water'. You could use a mnemonic to help you remember the causes of the February revolution.
- Some people revise well by listening, so you could try 'talking' your revision and recording it onto an mp3 player if you have one. Listen to these while lying in bed, while travelling in a car, or walking to the shops. This also takes the guilt out of being out and about rather than in front of your books!
- Practise your exam techniques. As you revise key topics, plan 5 or 6 points to make about the causes/ consequences/ key features / changes relating to major developments. You could use question stems 1–4 on the previous page, and slot in your own x and y.
- Try doing some timed essays. This will make it easier to write a good essay when it comes to the exam.
- Don't panic. Think about what you can achieve, not what you can't. Positive thinking is important! Remember the examiner will be looking to reward you for what you can do.

Assessment Objectives

To do well in your exam, you need to make sure you meet all the assessment objectives. Below are the assessment objectives you need to meet and some advice on how to make sure you meet them.

Recall, select and deploy historical knowledge

AO1a

In your essay, you must show that you can remember, choose and use historical knowledge.

- Remember – *recollect historical facts from your study of this unit*
- Choose – *select specific facts that are relevant to the essay you are writing*
- Use – *place these facts in your essay in a way that supports your argument*

Understanding of the past

AO1b (i)

You need to show that you understand the period studied. Simply telling the story of what happened will not help you to do this. Instead, you need to:

- Analyse – *break down the topic you are considering into key points*
- Explain – *suggest reasons why these key points provide an answer to the question*
- Reach a judgment – *Decide which of your key points was most important and provide reasons to support this*

As you think about analysis, explanation and judgment, remember to bear in mind the relevant **key concepts** and **relationships**.

Key concepts

AO1b (ii)

When faced with an essay question, consider which of the following key concepts it focuses on:

- Causation – *what made an event happen?*
- Consequence – *what were the results of this event?*
- Continuity – *in what ways did things stay the same?*
- Change – *in what ways were things different?*
- Significance – *why was this important?*

Then ensure that your answer remains focused on this concept.

Relationships

AO1b (iii)

Once you have planned the key points you will make in your essay, consider the following:

- How do these key points link together?
- Which key point was most important? Why?

Once you have considered these issues, arrange your points in an order that reflects the way they link together or the relative importance of each key point.

Level descriptors

Each essay you write in the exam will be given a mark out of 30 and will correspond to a level from 1 to 5, with level 5 being the highest. Here is some information about what the levels mean. Read it carefully and use this information to aim for the top!

Level 1:

- General points about the historical period that are correct but not necessarily focused on the topic raised by the question.
- The general points will not be supported by accurate and relevant specific examples.

Answers at this level will be very simplistic, irrelevant or vague.

Level 2:

- A number of general points about the topic of the question.
- The general points will be supported by some accurate and relevant examples.

Answers at this level might tell the story or part of the story without addressing the question, or might list the key points without backing them up with specific examples.

Level 3:

- A number of points with some focus on the question
- The points will be supported by accurate material, but some whole paragraphs may be either only partly relevant, lacking in detail or both.

At level 3 answers will attempt to focus on the question and have some strengths (some paragraphs will have point, supporting evidence and linkage back to the question), but answers will also have significant areas of weakness. For example, the focus on the question may drift, the answer may lack specific examples or parts of the essay may simply tell the story.

Level 4:

- A number of points which clearly address the question and show an understanding of the most important factors involved.
- The points will be supported by accurate material which will be mostly relevant and detailed.
- There will be clear explanation of how the points and specific examples provide an answer to the question.

At level 4 answers will clearly attempt to tackle the question and demonstrate a detailed knowledge of the period studied.

Level 5:

- A number of points which clearly answers the question and show a thorough understanding of the most important factors involved.
- The points will be supported by accurate material which will be relevant and detailed.
- There will be clear explanation of how the points and specific examples provide an answer to the question, as well as an evaluation of the relative importance of the different factors or issues discussed.

Answers that are judged to be level 5 will be thorough and detailed – they will clearly engage with the specific question providing a balanced and carefully reasoned argument that reaches a clear and supported judgment.

Sample answer 1

How far is it accurate to say that Nicholas II was personally responsible for his own downfall in February 1917? [30 marks available]

An answer given a mark in Level 4 of the published mark scheme.

In March 1917, Nicholas II abdicated as Tsar of Russia. In doing so he brought to an end 300 years of rule by his family and inaugurated the creation of a Russian Republic. The immediate cause of Nicholas II's downfall was a series of demonstrations, in February 1917, centred in the capital Petrograd, over food shortages which escalated into open criticism of the Tsar and his government. In many ways Nicholas II could be hold personally responsible for his own downfall, because in the preceding months he had failed to deal with the political and economic problems which faced his country.

EXAMINER COMMENT

The introductory paragraph places Nicholas II's fall in historical context. It highlights the immediate cause of his fall. It also links this to the focus of the question - the personal responsibility of Nicholas II in this development.

When he became Tsar, in 1894, Nicholas II seemed to be suited to the task he faced. Unlike his predecessor, Alexander III, Nicholas lacked strength of character and judgment to rule a vast empire facing major political and economic problems. Russia in the late 19th and early 20th centuries was regarded as economically and politically backward compared to other European Great Powers. Russia was still an overwhelmingly agricultural state where political power was firmly in the hands of the Tsar. Nicholas II's failure to address the problems faced by Russia was, in part, responsible for the outbreak of revolution in Russia in 1905. Nicholas II survived the revolution having made timely political concessions with the creation of Russia's first nationally elected parliament. However, Russia was still regarded as a state which engaged in political repression and faced economic problems in the towns and countryside. So by 1914, Nicholas II seemed to be ill suited to meet the challenges faced by the Russian state.

EXAMINER COMMENT

This second paragraph appears not to link directly with the question, but it is saved by the last sentence. Although the paragraph begins with a statement about Nicholas II and his ability as Tsar, it is written in a narrative style for the most part. However relevant comments are made about the personal abilities of Nicolas, and they are supported with evidence which shows that Russia's problems did not begin with Nicholas II. It concludes by linking this information back to the question and Nicholas's suitability as Tsar. The work would be even stronger if the paragraph had begun with a clear point either about Russia's problems or about Nicholas' personality and abilities. The student has written this paragraph without being t quite sure what its driving point is.

Of greater significance was Nicholas II's decision to enter the First World War, in July 1914. It was ultimately Nicholas's personal decision to intervene.The First World War placed great strains on the Russian economy which ultimately resulted in food shortages and demonstrations which led to demands for the Tsar's removal by the end of February 1917.

EXAMINER COMMENT

This short paragraph has a direct focus on the question. It has an analytical approach, better than the mainly descriptive approach of the paragraph before. It concentrates on the reasons for the downfall of the Tsar and

Nicholas II's personal role in that development. It links Nicholas clearly with a development which had a significant role in the fall of the Romanov dynasty.

In September 1915, Nicholas II made the fateful decision to become the commander of the Russian army on the Eastern Front. From that date forth all Russian defeats in its war with Germany and Austria-Hungary would be directly attributable to the Tsar himself. Following the failure of the Brusilov offensive in 1916 the Russian army faced defeat. As the Russian army retreated eastward support for the Tsar fell and desertions and mutinies within the army increased. So by February 1917 the Tsar's reputation for leadership had been greatly compromised.

EXAMINER COMMENT

This paragraph builds on the argument offered in the previous paragraph. It links Nicholas II's decision directly with Russian military defeat. It offers a direct link between a decision by Nicholas and his own downfall. The student's answer has become analytical.

While the Tsar was away at the front he left control of the government in the hands of his wife, the Tsarina Alexandra. She was not suited to leading the government through the crises caused by the demands for war. In attempting to deal with the issues of government the Tsarina was seen to rely heavily upon the advice of a holy man, Gregory Rasputin. Government instability was blamed directly on the Tsarina and Rasputin, and indirectly toward the Tsar himself.

EXAMINER COMMENT

Here the answer is drifting back into narrative description. A clear driving point is lacking. The last sentence links the material to the question, but rather implicitly. The paragraph is attempting to link Nicholas II with problems on the Home Front in Russia in the First World War. The argument that Nicholas II's decision to place his wife head of the government had a major effect on growing opposition to the Tsar and his government could have been made more forcefully at the beginning of the paragraph, giving the paragraph a clear driving point.

However, to see the Tsar as personally responsible for his own downfall is over simplistic. The problems facing the Russian state in terms of both political repression and economic development pre-dated his accession to power. The issues his faced domestically, as Tsar, were not of his making although he was ill prepared to deal effectively with them. Also, the decline in support for his government from September 1915 to February 1917 was more to do with his wife and her reliance on Rasputin's advice. In fact, the Tsar, in his correspondence with his wife after September 1915, counseled her against following Rasputin's views.

EXAMINER COMMENT

The command instruction for this question is 'how far'. This requires an answer which offers a balanced analysis of the assertion in the question. The first part of the response assesses the personal role of Nicholas II. This paragraph introduces other factors which explain the fall of the Tsar.

In addition, the poor performance of the Russian Army on the Eastern Front pre-dated Nicholas II's decision to take personal command of the armed forces. Russian forces had suffered heavy defeats at the hands of both the German and Austro-Hungarian armies in late 1915 and early 1915. In fact, in 1916, in the Brusilov offensive Russian forces temporarily made advances on the Eastern Front. Therefore, Nicholas II's role needs to be viewed against these other problems facing the Russian state.

EXAMINER COMMENT

This paragraph continues an appraisal of factors, other than the personal role of the Tsar, in his downfall. It points out that Nicholas II's personal command of the army did not cause Russian military defeat. This paragraph is well focused on the question.

Clearly, as the dominant political figure within the Russian state, Nicholas II deserves considerable blame for his own downfall. His personal characteristics of indecision and inability to deal directly with political and economic problems were a major factor in the ultimate downfall of the Romanov dynasty by March 1917. His decision to take personal command of the army stands out as a major reason for the rise in opposition to the Tsar's rule. However, Nicholas II's downfall must be seen within the context of the pressures placed on Russia as a result of participation in the First World War. The impact of war had profound effects on other participants in the war such as Germany and Austria-Hungary. Therefore, Nicholas II was an extremely important factor in the downfall of Tsarism, but to claim he was personally responsible for his own downfall is an exaggeration.

EXAMINER COMMENT

This concluding paragraph brings together the arguments put forward within the body of the response. It highlights the role of the Tsar and states that he was to a large extent personally responsible for his own downfall. However, it also shows that factors contributed to the Tsar's fall, thus beginning to offer a balanced analytical response to the question.

This response was awarded a mark in Level 4 of the mark scheme [19-24 marks.] The answer demonstrates explicit understanding of the question. The analysis is supported by accurate, relevant and appropriately selected factual material and it brings in a range of issues. However, the direct focus on the question was not always maintained and the short-term reasons for Nicholas' downfall are not fully explored. Although Nicholas' personal failings are shown well, the answer could have been improved with more examination of the other factors which led to Nicholas' downfall, with more supporting evidence to show the strains the war placed on the Russian economy. As a result, this response was awarded a high Level 4 mark of 23 and not Level 5.

Sample answer 2

How far is it accurate to say that Nicholas II was personally responsible for his own downfall in February 1917? [30 marks available]

An answer given a mark in Level 3 of the published mark scheme.

Nicholas II was ruler of Russia from 1894 to 1917. In that period Russia faced many problems. In 1905 it experienced revolution which lasted for almost a year. From 1914-1917 Russia was involved in the First World War. Nicholas II found dealing with Russia's political and economic problems extremely difficult and, in March 1917 he decided to abdicate from the position of Tsar.

EXAMINER COMMENT

The introduction is generally focused on the issue in the question. However, it is written in a descriptive-narrative way without an explicit link to the question.

Russia, in Nicholas II's reign was plagued by a variety of problems. Russia was a backward country in economic terms, compared to other major European states. Many Russians lived in poverty and faced harsh working conditions. Also Russia under Nicholas II had only limited political freedom.

Most political power was in the hands of the Tsar, so he was ultimately responsible for what happened in the political system.

EXAMINER COMMENT

This paragraph offers a background to the problem facing Nicholas II, but again with no direct linkage to the question. It provides historical context for a possible analysis of Nicholas II's personal role in his own downfall.

In 1905 Nicholas II almost fell from power in the 1905 Revolution. Russia was affected by widespread strikes and peasant uprisings. Nicholas II only survived because he issued to October Manifesto of 1905 which announced the creation of Russia's first elected national parliament. However, after 1905 Nicholas II's government still engaged in widespread political oppression against the revolutionaries of 1905 and other political radicals.

EXAMINER COMMENT

This paragraph offers a narrative description of important events in the reign of Nicholas II. However, it does not state clearly any assessment of Nicholas II's personal responsibility for his fall. Instead it refers to Nicholas II's role in keeping himself in power.

By the beginning of August 1914 Russia decided to enter the First World War. The war began well for Russia. Her armies entered the eastern part of Germany and conquered a large area of eastern Austria-Hungary. However, at the Battle of Tannenberg, in September 1914, the Russians were heavily defeated by the German Army. In 1915 the Russian suffered further defeats at Lodz and in the Gorlice-Tarnow offensive. So, in September 1915, the Tsar took personal command of the army. In Early 1916 Russia's position in the war began to improve. In the summer of 1916 the Brusilov offensive, by the Russians, won back territory on the Eastern Front. However, this change was short-lived. By the end of 1916 the Russian army was again in retreat and the Tsar received a lot of the blame.

EXAMINER COMMENT

This paragraph continues a narrative chronology of Nicholas II's reign. It offers evidence why Nicholas II's reign faced major problems as a result of entry into the First World War. In the final sentence it offers a brief link to the question with a comment on how the war had an adverse effect on the Tsar's rule.

On the Home Front in Russia the war had a major impact. Food prices rose and the main cities faced major food shortages. Ordinary Russians blamed the government. From September 1915, while the Tsar was at the Front, the government was under the control of the Tsar's wife, Alexandra. She was ill-suited to the task of running the government. To make matters worse she took advice from a holy man, Rasputin, which was greatly disliked by government officials and the Russian public.

EXAMINER COMMENT

This paragraph offers evidence of the impact of the war on Russia. It implies that Alexandra and Rasputin were at least partly to blame for the increasing unpopularity of the Tsar's government.

In February 1917, a demonstration, in Petrograd, to celebrate International Women's Day soon became a demonstration against food shortages. This, in turn, became a demonstration against the government. When troops were called in to suppress the demonstrations, many soldiers refused to obey orders. By the end of February government control of Petrograd was collapsing. In an attempt to restore his authority Nicholas II decided to return to Petrograd from the Front. Unfortunately, his train was halted by striking railwaymen at Pskov. There he met members of the Russian national parliament or Duma. They persuaded him to resign.

EXAMINER COMMENT

This paragraph offers a description of the main events in the capital Petrograd and in north Russia which resulted in the Tsar's downfall. There is no explicit link between the factual material presented and the question.

Therefore, to an extent, Nicholas II was responsible for his own downfall. His regime was repressive. Also his decision to take personal command of the army undermined his own authority and his decision to make Tsarina Alexandra head of the government made matters worse on the Home Front.

EXAMINER COMMENT

The final paragraph offers a clear link to the question and an attempt to assess directly the personal role of the Tsar in his own downfall. There is direct reference to the Tsar's role and the role of others such as the Tsarina. However, assessment is limited. It is focused specifically on events in the First World War.

This response was awarded a mark in Low Level 3 of the Mark Scheme [13-18 marks]. The answer demonstrates some understanding of the focus of the question and includes material which is narrative-descriptive and implicitly linked to the question's focus. On occasion it does stray from the question. The factual information provided is accurate but it not always used relevantly.

As a result, this response was awarded a low Level 3 Mark of 14 marks out of a possible 3o marks. It could be improved with more direct linkage of information to the question.

Index